Diet Intervention and Autism

Implementing the Gluten Free and Casein Free Diet for Autistic Children and Adults – A Practical Guide for Parents

Marilyn Le Breton

Foreword by Rosemary Kessick

Jessica Kingsley Publishers
London and Philadelphia

Every effort has been made to ensure that the information contained in this book is correct. The author does not take any responsibility for any changes to the information or for any decision taken as a result of this information.

The author does not endorse, approve or assume responsibility for any product, brand or company. The presence (or absence) of a product does not constitute approval (or disapproval) by the author. All information regarding food products and manufacturing is based upon information supplied by manufacturers and not based upon independent testing.

None of the information contained within the book is to be taken as medical advice. Always consult a medical practitioner before implementing any dietary intervention.

This book has been designed for use within the United Kingdom. If it is being used outside the United Kingdom, extra care will be needed, as information contained within the book may not be applicable.

First published in the United Kingdom in 2001
by Jessica Kingsley Publishers
116 Pentonville Road
London N1 9JB, UK
and
400 Market Street, Suite 400
Philadelphia, PA 19106, USA

www.jkp.com

Copyright © Marilyn Le Breton 2001
Foreword Copyright © Rosemary Kessick 2001

The right of Marilyn Le Breton to be identified as author of this work has been asserted by her in accordance with the Copyright, Designs and Patents Act 1988.

Library of Congress Cataloging in Publication Data
A CIP catalog record for this book is available from the Library of Congress

British Library Cataloguing in Publication Data
A CIP catalogue record for this book is available from the British Library

ISBN 978 1 85302 935 6

Printed and Bound in Great Britain by
Athenaeum Press, Gateshead, Tyne and Wear

Contents

Acknowledgements

There are many, many people who have helped me with this book and this is the only chance I get to acknowledge this publicly and thank them.

So my heartfelt thanks to:

My Mum, for proofreading this and for a lifetime of unwavering support.

Dr Mike Tettenborn – of all the paediatricians in all the world, Jack and I were lucky enough to find you.

All at Allergy induced Autism, especially Rosemary Kessick and Meryll Nee. The debt that I and so many other families of autistic children owe you is vast and never likely to be repaid. Please keep on battling away on behalf of our children.

Jessica Kingsley Publishers, especially Helen Parry, for having faith in the diet and confidence in me.

The staff of Henry Tyndale School nursery and reception classes, for being an amazing group of dedicated, caring individuals, for their unqualified support of Jack's diet and for bravely testing out the cake and biscuit recipes in this book.

All the specialist suppliers and manufacturers listed in the book, for all their time and the help that they gave me in compiling the correct information regarding their gf/cf products.

Lisa Lewis, whose book *Special Diets for Special Kids* helped me so much in the early days of the diet and indirectly inspired me to write this.

Barbara Powell of Barbara's Kitchen, whose enthusiasm for baking nearly rubbed off on me, and who has managed to show me that gf/cf baking is not only possible, but can taste wonderful.

Genetta, for caring enough and sending me a newspaper clipping about AiA and the gf/cf diet and in so doing, setting in motion the whole train of events which have enabled me to help my son, Jack.

All the dedicated parents I've spoken to about the diet, who are so determined to help their children.

Very special thanks must go to my son Luke, who has chomped his way, uncomplaining, through so many different versions of the recipes in this book (and many which did not make it), until I got them right.

This book is dedicated with my deepest love to my two wonderful sons, Luke and Jack. These two unique people have each, in their own way, taught me so much about myself and the world around me. I am for ever indebted to them.

Foreword

'There is no evidence to support the theory that dietary regimes can help children on the autistic spectrum.'

This is the common reaction of so many GPs and specialists when they are approached for advice and help with dietary intervention.

So what exactly is evidence? Well, in my dictionary it's defined as: '…indication, sign, clearness, facts in support of…information tending to establish the facts…'. Thousands of children and adults on the autistic spectrum demonstrate spectacular and permanent changes once their diet is altered and those problems, once forgotten, often return abruptly when the diet is infringed. Evidence enough to the many, many parents whose children now sleep through the night, say 'Mummy' and 'Daddy' for the first time and start noticing the world around them.

In medic speak, they may mean no *scientific* evidence; no abundance of medical papers on the subject each re-iterating the point. It is, of course, quite right and proper to be cautious, and it's true to say that there isn't a glut of medical papers on the subject, but why should that be?

Where does most of the funding come from for medical research? From commercial enterprises, and what incentive is there for any commercial company to prove that the staple foods of the Western diet are damaging to our ASD children?

To their immense credit, there are still stoic researchers round the world, doggedly committed to seeking the answers despite the lack of funding for their work. Long before most of our children were born, indeed before AiA was born, a great Norwegian, Dr Karl Reichelt expounded the theories of opioid excess. With a number of studies published in respectable medical journals he collaborated in an impressive five-year educational study into the effects of a gluten and casein free diet on ASD children. More recently, Dr Rosemary Waring at Birmingham University identified faulty biochemistry which can lead many ASD sufferers to react adversely to a whole range of foods, household chemicals and drugs.

These scientists, together with many UK and overseas colleagues, have been key to the broad understanding we now have of why many ASD children and adults react so catastrophically to something as common-place as food.

There are other reasons why so many GPs and paediatricians are so reticent to accept that diet can be a factor in helping their patients. Autism has traditionally fallen within the remit of psychologists and psychiatrists, which may deter some doctors from considering potential physiological aspects to the condition. In some autistic people, about two per cent, their condition is already known to be associated with a metabolic disease, virus or bacterial infection, or a genetic disorder.

Almost everyone you talk to these days is touched by autism and fright-ening statistics are emerging which back up the perception that there is a huge increase in cases. The gene pool doesn't change rapidly, so the finger of suspicion points at the environment. There remain many unanswered questions as to the origin of the problem, but if doctors only treated the symptoms of diseases when they knew, without a doubt, what had caused them, then the surgeries of the land would be pretty empty!

When you first hear the word **autism** applied to your child, your blood runs cold. Then, when the good doctors who have just delivered the news to you bow out of the picture with a 'wait and see' attitude, where do you turn? What do you do?

Sadly, many people spend a great deal of money searching for the best way to help their child when the answer is right there, under their noses, all the time. It doesn't have to cost a great deal and it can turn your world right around, as it did for Marilyn and her family. Marilyn's sensible, no-nonsense approach leads you through the maze of dietary advice, equipping you with a clear map of precautions and ideas, all well researched, factual and informative yet still presented with her mischie-vous sense of humour!

I owe Marilyn an enormous debt of gratitude for her perseverance and dedication in writing this book, which will enable so many more parents take the step which could improve their ASD child's quality of life beyond measure.

Rosemary CT Kessick
CEO, Allergy induced Autism, January 2001

Introduction

You have probably already heard a lot about the gluten free and casein free (gf/cf) diet for autistic children. There have been many moving personal stories about the amazing changes that have occurred in an autistic child who has been placed on this diet. You are just as likely to have heard (or more probably imagined) how difficult, time-consuming, limiting and expensive the diet is. I hope that this book will dispel those myths, along with any other misconceptions that you may have, and give you the confidence and the knowledge that you will need to implement the diet successfully with your child.

I know from my own experience that the thought of the gf/cf diet is at best daunting; I was terrified. I knew about the diet for six months before I implemented it with my son, Jack. I now bitterly regret these wasted months.

During this time, I knew that I had to give the diet a go. The more I read about the theory behind it, the more sense it made to me. Not only did it appear to be tailor-made for Jack, but it also seemed that it would not cause any major problems for the rest of the family. It seemed the most sensible route of treatment to try with him. It did not involve giving him drugs (that I had already decided would be the last resort, but I felt we could be rapidly heading that way), nor did it involve very intensive behavioural treatments. I have nothing against such programmes, but I was far too worn down to fight for funding, get trained, recruit the people needed to run a programme and face the possibility of further disruption to what was an already disrupted household.

Yet despite all of my rationalisation, I still could not get around to implementing the diet. It just seemed too hard to get to grips with. I simply didn't feel that I was up to the task. I was exhausted, as Jack rarely slept. On a good night, I would get two or three hours of broken sleep.

Sometimes I didn't sleep at all. The days with Jack were similarly exhausting.

As well as having an autistic child (and you know only too well what that involves) and trying to run a house (something that I show no natural aptitude for), Jack's older brother, Luke, is Down Syndrome. With two special needs children under five and little sleep, I felt that there was no way I could get to grips with the diet, find out what needed to be done and then do it.

To those who know me well, it came as little surprise that when I finally did decide to start the diet, I went about it like the proverbial bull in a china shop. I jumped straight in and did not give any thought to trying to get prepared properly. I just started the diet by removing all the foods that I knew Jack should not eat, and only then did I start to try to find out what I could feed Jack with. I made life so hard for myself and so unnecessarily difficult for Jack. I also made mistakes. Oh boy, did I make some mistakes.

So in essence, this is the book which I wish I could have read in those months prior to starting the diet. Then, perhaps, I would not have wasted so much time getting around to implementing the diet with Jack. Maybe such a book would have prevented me from making so many silly mistakes. Maybe too, I could have found the gf/cf food (the cheaper, good-quality and easy to obtain gf/cf food) which I needed for Jack straight away, instead of initially feeding him gf/cf bread that wasn't even fit for the birds and spending months and far too much money on unsuitable foods that ended up in the bin and on phone calls to food manufacturers and suppliers, trying to locate all the things that I needed for him.

I do need to point out, right from the start, a few things.

The first is that I haven't included a case study about Jack, before and on the diet. This book isn't about Jack. It is about helping you to implement the diet, so that you can help your child. Each child is so different. How Jack was and how he is now is irrelevant. I fear that if I go into great detail about how Jack's autism presented itself and how the diet changed him, you may well not see any similarities between Jack and your child and you may feel that the diet will be of no benefit to your child. This is not the case. I truly believe that every child, wherever they might be on the autistic spectrum, can be helped by this diet. Having said that there is no case study of Jack, that does not mean that Jack doesn't get mentioned – he does. I am very proud of him and of course I mention him, but usually to illustrate a point.

I also need to point out (or confess), that I loathe all forms of housework and that includes cooking. One of the things that prevented me from starting the diet earlier than I did was the thought that I would spend the rest of my life up to my elbows in flour. Cooking is still not my favourite way of passing the time, but the little baking that I now do, I do from choice.

I am, unfortunately, not related to the Rothschilds, nor do I have a trust fund, so I do this diet on the cheap. Some items on the diet do cost more than 'normal' food, but as with everything else, there are usually ways around this. Basically, what I am trying to point out is that if I can do this diet successfully, then everyone else can. I hope you are just about to prove that for yourself.

The final point that I need to make is that I am guilty of saying the same things many times. I make no apologies for this. Some things about this diet are so important that it is worth repeating them, to make sure that they are hammered home. Also, I appreciate that you may read this book from cover to cover initially, but if you refer to it in the future, just to dip into, to check something, I'd hate you to miss something important, just because I'd referred to it elsewhere in the book and didn't want to repeat it again.

I have tried to cover all the basics of the gf/cf diet in as much depth as possible, in order to make the diet as easy, straightforward and pain free as it truly is. I hope that this book will encourage you to start the diet and that the changes that your child experiences once on the diet will be all the encouragement that you need to continue with it.

I wish you, and your child, all the very best.

The Diet

What Exactly is This Diet All About?

The basis of the diet is very simple and straightforward. All you need to do is to remove four things from your child's diet: gluten, casein, mono-sodium glutamate and aspartame.

Gluten is a protein that is found in four types of cereals: wheat, rye, barley and oats. That's it. All other types of cereals and grains can be included on the diet.

The only tricky thing about a gluten free diet is that in the western world, the majority of the flour that is used in food production comes from wheat. But if panic is starting to creep in, try not to worry; there are lots and lots of different types of flour that can be safely used instead. And if you don't want to use gluten free flours to cook and bake with, stay relaxed, because there are an awful lot of companies out there who are using these flours to create food that is gluten free, and you can buy that.

Casein is the protein that is found in milk – all animal milks, not just cow's milk. So instead of swapping from cow's milk over to sheep or goat milk, you will need to get 'milk' from a non-animal source. The variety of milk substitutes is huge. There are soya milks in a variety of flavours, rice milk, almond milk, potato milk and even 'milk' made from sunflower oil and pea protein! Most of these milks (especially the soya milks) are very easy to obtain at your local supermarket.

Monosodium glutamate is a chemical that is added to some foods and drinks to enhance the flavour of the food. It disguises the less palatable (and even downright awful) tastes in a food and magnifies the pleasant tastes. There really is no need for this to be in food in the first place. If a food or drink doesn't taste nice, why should someone try to convince us it does, by adding chemicals? Why don't they just make nicer-tasting food in the first place?

Aspartame is the group name given to some artificial sweeteners. Once again there is no need for our children to be eating and drinking substances that contain aspartame.

The reasons for excluding these four items from our children's diets will be explained in greater detail further on in the book. But that is the diet in a nutshell. All it involves is the removal of four things from your child's diet.

If you are panicking that this is all far too difficult, please try to remember these four points:

1. Gluten is avoided by thousands and thousands of people in the UK alone. Add up all the people who are intolerant to gluten around the world, and the number is in the millions. Not only do coeliacs need to avoid gluten (currently 1 in 1000 people have been medically diagnosed as coeliac), but also so do those who suffer from dermatitis herpetiformis. Also there are members of the general population who are sensitive to gluten and for whom it causes a variety of problems. If you remove gluten from your child's diet, he or she will be joining a sizeable part of the wider community.

2. Four-fifths of the world's population are unable to tolerate milk. Usually this is due to an inability to digest lactose, the naturally occurring sugar in milk. Milk is also the most common source of allergy in children under five years of age. Avoidance of milk and all of its byproducts is often recommended to those who suffer from asthma and eczema. Vegans by virtue of their beliefs do not eat or drink anything that originates from animals, so that obviously includes milk. Your child will hardly be in the minority if you remove milk from their diet.

3. Monosodium glutamate and aspartame are fairly new products. The human diet has managed very successfully without them in the past and there is much evidence to show that we would all be better off without them in our diet now.

4. I managed to do the diet with my son. There is nothing special or superhuman about me. If I, and thousands of other parents in the UK, have managed to implement the diet, you can too!

Why should you remove gluten, casein, monosodium glutamate and aspartame from your child's diet? Read on…

The Opioid Excess Theory

My son, Jack, is a drug addict.

He has been a drug addict for a long time, but I only discovered it, or more truthfully, had the courage to face it, when he was three and a half years old. The chances are, your autistic child is a drug addict too.

I realise that I have just made a bold, shocking and sweeping statement. There are lots of small medical studies whose findings support what I have said (see Further Reading for more details), but unfortunately, so far, there have been no large, long-term studies that will make the medical professionals who treat our children sit up and take notice. But in all honesty, I really don't care about this 'lack of concrete evidence'. For me and hundreds of other parents of autistic children in Britain and many thousand more parents in Europe and the United States, this medical proof is not necessary. We have all the proof we need; we have back the child we never knew we had lost.

Unfortunately, as the word of parents (the people who know their child the best), is rarely taken as evidence, let alone proof, the title of this section will have to remain, for the time being, 'The Opioid Excess Theory'. What follows is the theory behind the diet; the basic, brief and my very unscientific version of the theory (I am sorry, but I don't 'do' science). For those of you who have more than 'O' level Biology, I apologise in advance. If you require further, in-depth information, please see the later section on Further Reading for the relevant scientific papers. Remember, what you are about to read is for the moment, all theory.

When you eat, the food you consume is broken down in your stomach. The bits that are not used by the body are flushed out as waste matter. In autistic people, the breakdown of two proteins present in some foods, gluten and casein, is not completed properly. The resulting fragments of these proteins are called peptides. Peptides are small enough to pass through the wall of the gut, rather than being processed in the normal way. The autistic individuals who are producing these peptides are likely to have gut walls that are damaged and therefore these peptides find it even easier to pass through them. These peptides get into the bloodstream and the central nervous system. As the peptides journey around the body, they make a pit stop at the brain, where they do untold damage before continuing their journey and finally making their way out of the body, via urine.

It is worth noting at this point that the gf/cf diet should not be confused with coeliac disease. Although coeliacs also eliminate gluten from their diet (they can tolerate casein), they do so because they can hardly break down gluten at all. The protein remains in large pieces and as a result, stays in the gut and does severe damage to the gut wall.

So why is Jack a drug addict?

The protein, gluten, breaks down into the peptide gluteomorphine and the milk protein, casein, breaks down into the peptide caseomorphine. You've probably already worked out for yourself that both of these peptides are very similar to morphine, a highly addictive drug.

This is the theory. My understanding of biology is slight. But compared to that of some people I come into contact with who want to know why Jack is on such a weird diet, it is positively masterful. I quickly noticed in the early days of the diet that when I answered their question with the scientific explanation, it didn't take long before I would see their eyes glaze over and feel that they were silently regretting having asked me. So, I usually tell another version of the opioid excess theory: a more entertaining, colourful and graphic version. What follows is the 'tabloid' version of the opioid excess theory.

Jack is a 'drug' addict. His body is unable to break down certain foods, primarily gluten, milk (who has ever heard of casein?), monosodium glutamate and aspartame (I'll deal with MSG and aspartame in a bit). Instead, his body converts them into morphine-like substances, which float around his body and brain, causing havoc.

Two-thirds of the time, Jack was as 'high as a kite', which accounted for his lack of eye contact, being in a world of his own, the sensory problems with his sight, his self-stimulation, his bizarre behaviours, his incredibly high pain threshold and his total lack of any sense of danger. When you consider that morphine is not only a highly addictive drug, but also the strongest pain killer known to man, gluteomorphine and caseomorphine would completely explain away all of the above.

The screaming fits that Jack had both day and night, when he would attack himself and me, occurred when the poor little mite was having the withdrawal symptoms from his drug. He was in pain and totally out of control. Which was why I had found that the easiest way to calm him down was to give him a glass of milk and a couple of biscuits or a bread roll. He had then had his drug 'fix' and he'd 'tune' out again and display all of his classic autistic tendencies. Jack's whole life revolved around being 'high' and going through withdrawal, several times a day.

If you find it hard to believe that a morphine high can be in any way related to autistic-like behaviours, you need only read an account of the experiences of a heroin addict to prove just how similar the two are. If you read a few of the many, many accounts of LSD and other hallucinogenic drug 'trips', you will be left with little doubt as to how the sensory problems our children experience can be related to powerful drugs.

This analogy also serves a purpose when dealing with those well-meaning relatives and friends who just haven't grasped how serious the situation is, and who think that you are potty for attempting the diet. For example, a relative of Jack's, who knew about the diet and who had best remain nameless, came round one day with a packet of chocolate buttons for each of the boys. I said that Jack couldn't have them because he was allergic to them and therefore Luke wouldn't have them while Jack was around (this was in the early days of the diet; Jack wouldn't touch them now). I was told by this nameless relative that 'one packet wouldn't hurt'. Yet again, I explained to the nameless one the story of Jack, the toddler drug addict. This time, out of sheer exasperation (how many times was I expected to explain this, before it sunk in?), I added that I would rather the nameless one make their way to the less salubrious part of town and purchase some heroin for Jack and help him mainline it. The nameless one quite rightly looked horrified (I began to imagine the calls to Childline, social services and the NSPCC) – surely I was joking? But I stood my ground and I explained that as far as I was concerned, the heroin would do Jack the same amount of harm as the packet of chocolate buttons. OK, I admit that this was a little OTT, but it did manage finally to drive the message home, in a way that I had never been able to do before, about how serious Jack's allergies are and how serious and committed to the diet I am. The point was taken and a few weeks later it had become completely redundant, when the same sceptical relative ('I think that this is a stupid idea. Poor Jack has got enough to try to cope with, without you making his life even more difficult' etc.), saw the massive change that had taken place in Jack. On this later visit, I was told, 'Who could have believed the difference this diet would make? It's wonderful, truly amazing. He's a completely different boy now.' I refrained from making any cutting remarks or even an understandable 'I told you so', and just smiled sweetly.

So, that is the theory behind the diet. I bet you are now itching to get started. Or are you still unsure/unconvinced? Don't worry, I was too. What really got me thinking more seriously about giving the diet a go was when I received some basic information from a marvellous charity group, Allergy induced Autism (AiA). I cannot urge you strongly enough to contact/join AiA (their details appear in Directory of Useful Contacts at the end of the book). For a start, they do the scientific stuff and they are an absolute goldmine of information. I could not have managed to implement Jack's diet half as successfully as I did without their help.

The following extract is printed with the kind permission of AiA.

Our AiA children often display one or more of the following:

- Hyperactivity
- Sleep problems
- Giggling/screaming for no apparent reason
- Excessive thirst
- Craving/dislike for certain foods
- Hot and sweaty, especially at night
- History of glue ear
- Eats non-foods, e.g. earth, sand, paper, soap
- Diarrhoea and/or constipation
- Swollen tummy

- Constantly breaking wind
- Constant catarrh/runny nose
- Inability to control temperature
- Red ears or face
- Dark shadows under the eyes
- Pale skin, pasty face
- Aches, cramps, tiredness
- Allergy in the family (asthma, eczema, hay fever, migraine)
- Gut disorders in the family (coeliac disease, Crohn's disease, ulcerative colitis, pernicious anaemia)

Does any of this sound familiar to you? When I read this, I was astounded. How could a group of people I had never met before and who didn't know Jack, describe him so accurately? With the exception of the glue ear, I could truthfully answer yes to every question. Things that I had taken for granted as 'just being Jack' or just being part of the autism, now seemed to be something different. They had to be. Even if you are a complete sceptic and charge AiA with highlighting so many things that your child is bound to relate to one of them, how would they know (and why did they think it so important) that one side of Jack's family (mine) could migraine for Britain (if they gave out gold medals for migraine, I'd have a display case full) and on the other side of the family, you'd be hard pressed to find someone that didn't have asthma, eczema and hay fever (all three, that is, in the same person), both in the immediate and the extended family? As for gut disorders (various types and of varying seriousness) both families could raise their hands and say 'Aye'. Pernicious anaemia – well I don't know if it is pernicious, but I can't remember a blood test of mine which has ever come back saying that I wasn't anaemic. My local blood donors' unit have got sick of waving me away (I have since been informed (thank you, Rosemary) that pernicious anaemia is a B12 disorder and not related to iron deficiency, but at the time it knocked me for six). When I got to the bit about the red ear, it is fair to say that I was stunned. How on earth could they know about Jack's intermittent red ear? I had for a very long time thought that Jack's red ear was caused by his night-time gouging, but recently I had noticed that it flared up and went away at the oddest of times, during the day. It soon afterwards became apparent that whenever Jack's ear (it was only ever the one ear at a time) went red, we were in for a bad time with Jack. It became the family's early warning system. If Jack's ear went red, we knew he was going to be uncontrollable and I privately wished that I had access to an old-fashioned suit of armour, as invariably I was going to get hurt. I swear to this day, if I hadn't read the bit about the red ear, I might still be thinking up good excuses not to attempt the diet. We all have our own 'road to Damascus' – this was mine. Luckily (?), this happened at the same time Jack was ill. Once again, he was barely eating. So rather than encourage and entice him into eating again all the things I was considering eliminating from his diet, I decided to start his diet right away. Not for me the careful planning that I'm just about to advise you to do. Oh no, as I've already said, I just jumped straight into the deep end. I would like to apologise publicly to Jack for doing so. Sorry son, with all the best intentions in the world, I cocked up big time. I got it right in the end and now I'm doing some very public penance.

I have stressed many times that the opioid excess theory is just that, a theory. If a lack of medical evidence is still putting you off trying the diet with your child, it shouldn't, for two very good reasons.

The first reason is that if you are waiting for concrete proof, you will probably wait/waste your child's entire lifetime. I can't see anyone stumping up the vast amount of money needed to undertake such a project. Call me a cynic, but there is no one out there who will benefit or gain from such research (except autistic people and their families). I can't see a pharmaceutical company (the organisations who would usually undertake such research), funding a study. They would have nothing to gain from it. The autistic person isn't going to be cured by a 'wonder-drug'. A study would only prove that a change in diet would help, and the drug companies are not going to benefit financially from that. In fact, they are likely to lose money, if parents follow the diet and take their children off the various medications that they have already been prescribed. The Government aren't going to do a study or provide the money for a medical facility to do it. If they did, it is highly likely the next question would be, why can't our children break down these proteins like other people? The answer to this would probably prove both embarrassing and financially costly, as the compensation claims started rolling in.

The only people who could possibly benefit from such a project would be food manufacturers, who could corner the market in providing tasty, wholesome, nutritious gf/cf food, but as other groups of people who follow special diets – coeliacs, diabetics, etc. – have been ignored for years by large food manufacturers and instead are catered for by small, specialist companies, I can't see them going out of their way to help either.

The second and most important reason is that you are reading this book. Unless you are reviewing it for a periodical (I should be so lucky!), you want to help your child. I would personally crawl over broken glass, in a room full of spiders, if I thought it would help my children. Luckily, I don't have to do that. Think about what you are actually proposing to do. All you are going to do is change your child's diet. Would you worry so much if you decided to feed your child a strict vegetarian diet? If you and your family are vegetarian, did you worry to the same extent about your child following the same diet? If your child were diabetic, would you delay following the appropriate diet? If you are an orthodox Jew or Muslim and don't live in a large city, you probably experience more problems getting kosher/halal food than you will getting gf/cf food. You are only modifying your child's diet. You are not pumping them full of chemicals or experimental drugs; you are not implementing a behavioural modification programme, which can be costly or intrusive for the rest of your family. You're not even clutching at straws, as you are following something hundreds and hundreds of other people have found beneficial. Surely it is worth trying for a few weeks to see if your child will benefit from it too?

Monosodium Glutamate and Aspartame

It's confession time. The diet is called the gluten free and casein free diet, but it should really be the 'gluten free, casein free, monosodium glutamate and aspartame free diet'. But it's a bit of a mouthful, so whenever I refer to the diet, I really mean monosodium glutamate (MSG) free and aspartame free, as well as being gluten free and casein free.

Why should MSG and aspartame be excluded from your child's diet?

Before I get to the science bit (remember, I don't 'do' science), a story/confession to illustrate the importance of removing MSG and aspartame.

Jack had been ill and was getting better. I decided that this was as good a time as any to withdraw gluten and casein from his diet. Eight days later, I was feeling pretty proud of myself. Eight days, and Jack had not eaten a thing containing gluten or casein. It wasn't the best eight days and nights we had spent together, but his withdrawal from gluten and casein was not as bad as I had been led to believe it would be. I was feeling very pleased with myself. So pleased, in fact, that I phoned Rosemary Kessick of AiA, to tell her (boast) how well Jack and I were doing.

In retrospect, I am very grateful to Rosemary for not calling me an irresponsible parent for going about the diet the way I did. Instead, she said very calmly, 'Hula Hoops!'

'Hula Hoops?' I replied; what was this woman talking about?

'You're feeding him Hula Hoops, aren't you?'

The penny dropped, I knew (thought I knew) what she was on about.

'Yes I am.' And I continued in my smuggest tone (I do a good line in smug!), 'But it's OK, they are the ready-salted ones. They are marked gluten free.' Did she really think I'd get caught out giving him flavoured crisps? I had done enough research to know that flavoured crisps were off limits now. I had been very grateful to the Hula Hoops. Jack was already self-restricting his diet so much without me restricting it even more. I had been pleased he could continue to eat Hula Hoops. In fact, he had eaten little else all week. One day he had eaten eight packets, to supplement his gf burger and chips.

I didn't hear Rosemary take a deep breath, but looking back, she must have done.

'They are gluten free, but they contain monosodium glutamate.'

She went on to explain that children on the gf/cf diet react badly to MSG and that I should remove it completely from Jack's diet, along with the gluten and casein. I did remove the MSG from his diet straight away and the next few days were hell. He had been getting some sort of 'fix' from MSG. I'd removed gluten and casein and like any true addict, he had got his 'fix' from another source. Not such a strong or long-lasting 'fix', but a 'fix' nevertheless. Which was why the first eight days of the diet were not as bad as I thought they would be.

It is just as well I am not too proud to boast. If I was, I'd never have phoned Rosemary, and who knows how long it would have been before I found out about the effects of MSG and took it out of Jack's diet.

The entire household has been free of MSG for several months now. The more I read about it, the unhappier I was giving it to Luke and even eating it myself. Aside from what it did to Jack, did I really want Luke and I to eat food whose true taste had to be disguised by an added flavour enhancer which tricked my brain into thinking it was tasty? Food is either tasty or it isn't. I didn't want to eat food that wasn't naturally delicious, so the house became an MSG free zone. Many months after being MSG free, I ate two bags of cheese and onion crisps (a lifelong weakness of mine, and Jack's and Luke's) one evening. They, of course, contained MSG. Despite being very tired, I couldn't sleep. I felt very on edge and jittery, as if I had spent the whole day consuming very strong coffee. If that is the effect that the MSG in two packets of crisps had on my body (a fully grown, healthy-ish, non-autistic adult), after my resistance to MSG had been lowered, what on earth had it been doing to Jack (or Luke, come to that)?

So what about aspartame?

I did not remove aspartame from Jack's diet for a very long time. I really didn't know that I needed to. In fact, it was not until I started to do some serious research for this book that I found out that aspartame belongs to the same group of chemicals as MSG. The minute I did find out, I made sure that this house became an aspartame free zone. Two strange and wonderful things happened.

The first was that, within a month, I had a different Jack – again! I had often said that I sometimes got a glimpse of another Jack, but it was only ever glimpses. I knew by now that it must be something to do with his diet, but I could never work out what it could be. Well that something was aspartame and now I have the Jack I occasionally saw, permanently.

The second thing that happened, completely unrelated to Jack (or is it?), is that my migraines stopped. Up until this point I would average two migraines a month (always one and sometimes up to eight). In six months, I have not had a single migraine. Again the more I've read about MSG and aspartame, the more I am convinced that they were a major contributing factor for my migraines. I used to be a complete glutton for cheese and onion crisps and diet cola drinks. I really miss the huge tubes of crisps that I would devour nightly, but it's a small price to pay for being migraine free.

Well, I can't put it off any longer. It's time to do the science bit.

Excitotoxins – Monosodium glutamate and aspartame

Monosodium glutamate is widely used as a flavour enhancer in many of the processed foods and drinks that we consume. Its job is to mask disagreeable tastes and magnify the agreeable ones. Alarmingly, in the last 50 years, the amount of MSG added to food has doubled every ten years.

Monosodium glutamate is the sodium salt of glutamic acid. Glutamate is found naturally in plant and animal tissues. Even human breast milk contains glutamate.

The Japanese first discovered that foods cooked in a stock made from a particular seaweed tasted far better than food cooked in other stocks. About a hundred years ago, a Japanese scientist located the substance in the seaweed stock that made the food taste so good. This substance was glutamic acid.

Today MSG is rarely made from seaweed. Instead it is most commonly derived from sugar beet or cane or more rarely, wheat.

Monosodium glutamate is one of a group of compounds known as an excitotoxin. Another excitotoxin that is commonly used in processed food is aspartame (an artificial sweetener, which goes under various trade names). Excitotoxins are most commonly present in processed foods and diet drinks. They are more toxic when they are present in a liquid form (soups, gravies, sauces and diet drinks) than when they are added to solid food. This is because the body absorbs them more quickly. Excitotoxins have been shown to react with certain receptors in the brain and kill off certain types of neurons.

The obvious question is, if glutamate is a substance that occurs naturally in the human body and brain, why can it harm the brain? The answer, in brief, is that the amount of glutamate that occurs naturally in the brain is minute. When the level of glutamate rises above this natural level, the brain's neurons begin to fire abnormally and when the glutamate reaches a high enough level, these brain cells undergo a process of delayed death, known as excitotoxity (they are literally excited to death). The more excitotoxins there are present in a food or drink, the more toxic the result.

It seems that food manufacturers are going to extraordinary lengths to disguise MSG in food. It can be known as E621, sodium hydrogen l-glutamate, flavour enhancer and aji-no-moto. It occurs naturally in all yeast extract and hydrolysed vegetable protein (HVP). It can also be present when the following are listed in the ingredients of food: vegetable protein, textured protein, soy protein extract, caseinate and natural flavouring.

Cautionary note: When these appear on the ingredients list, do not automatically presume that they include MSG; it is better to contact the food manufacturer and ask the source of the ingredient. By doing this, not only will you prevent yourself from taking more food items out of your child's diet than you need to, but also you will send a very clear message to food manufacturers that our children have a problem with MSG. You never know, if enough of us phone, they might even stop using the stuff!

So why do MSG and other excitotoxins such as aspartame have such an effect on our children? There have been no big medical studies on MSG and autism, but it appears that along with their inability to process gluten and casein properly, our children are hypersensitive to certain additives. If you don't want to take my word for it, take MSG and aspartame out of your child's diet and see the difference for yourself.

It isn't just me or other parents with children on the diet who are worried about the effect of MSG. The use of glutamates in baby foods was voluntarily discontinued in the United Sates in 1970, after it was found that the glutamate could induce brain damage in an immature brain. It is likewise recommended in America that aspartame should not be used in food designed for babies and young children.

There are some fascinating (and scary) research documents about MSG, aspartame, glutamates and other excitotoxins, details of which can be found under Further Reading at the end of the book.

Misconceptions and Commonly Asked Questions about the Diet

Since I began the diet with Jack, I have had many phone calls from parents of autistic children, who have either just started the diet or who are thinking of doing so. Those who have started the diet usually want either to check that they are following it correctly, get some more information, or more often than not, track down an acceptable gf/cf alternative food for their child. You will find the answers to these questions, I hope, in the following chapters. Those parents who are thinking of starting the diet or who have already decided to do so usually ask the same sorts of questions. So if you fall into this category, please read on.

The diet is too difficult and time consuming

I truly believe that this is the biggest hurdle to overcome. I hear it time and time again. And I know all about it. I believed this so wholeheartedly that it prevented me from starting the diet for six months.

The whole reason for writing this book was to make the diet as straightforward and as easy to follow as possible. If I have managed to do this, by the time you have finished reading the book you will be exuding so much self-confidence and knowledge that, if the diet doesn't seem a breeze, it will at least be a much easier task than you had previously thought.

So, is the diet time consuming?

Yes it is, is the honest answer. But only in the very beginning. Like anything else that is new, it does take time to learn about it, understand it and then some more time to adjust to it. It very soon becomes second nature. It does, really. For the first few weeks, the weekly shop will take a bit longer, as you check the ingredients on the food you are buying for your child, to see if it is gf/cf.

A bit of planning in advance will help. If you generally buy the majority of your groceries from one supermarket, you will be able to check in advance the supermarket's own brand items that are gf/cf. All the super-markets provide comprehensive lists of their own brand items that are gluten and milk free. All you have to do is phone them (telephone numbers for all the major supermarket chains and food manufacturers are supplied in the Directory of Useful Contacts at the back of the book) and ask for the lists to be sent to you. You can then check those items you usually buy or would like to buy, to see if they are suitable. Unfortunately, few of the supermarkets at the time of printing provide lists for food containing MSG or aspartame. But please ask them for it anyway. If enough people ask, they just might start providing one. And if enough people point out to them that there is a problem relating to these two substances, they might one day stop using them (that's my idealistic streak talking).

On the bright side, Iceland's own-brand items do not contain artifi-cially added MSG, artificial colourings or flavourings (including aspartame) or genetically modified food. They have also managed to produce one booklet which covers a whole range of allergies, including gluten and milk. If one supermarket can do this without its shareholders rising up in revolt, perhaps other supermarkets will follow their example.

As I have said, the diet soon becomes second nature. It really is like learning to drive a car. If you think back to the first few lessons you had, the pre-driving checks took up more of the lesson time than the actual driving did. The next few lessons saw you being a hazard to other road users, as you were very nervous and overly cautious. Now driving is second nature. You get in the car and head off for your destination. The mechanics of driving the car are not given a second thought; instead you concentrate on the traffic.

Shopping for the gf/cf diet is just like that. The first few trips to the supermarket will see you spending more time looking at the ingredients labels of foods than actually putting food in the trolley. This does have its compensations. I am now on first-name terms with most of the store detec-tives in my local supermarket! On the next few trips, you will have a good knowledge of most of the foods you can buy for the diet, but you will still be a little hesitant. You still double check the food you bought last week or linger over a few new items to see if they are acceptable (whether you plan to buy them or not). A few weeks later, the shopping has once again become the repetitive and mundane chore that it always has been. In fact, don't be surprised if a year into the diet, you look back at those first few weeks of shopping for gf/cf food with a rosy glow of nostalgia. At least shopping was a bit interesting then. All right, so I'm exaggerating with that last comment, but it really doesn't take very long for the diet to become as much a part of the life of your family as everything else is at the moment. If a super slob like me can do it, then I'm afraid that everyone else can too.

Is the diet difficult?

No, it isn't. Seriously, it isn't. It isn't difficult; it is just different. Things that are different from the way we normally do things always seem difficult. It is no harder than deciding to become vegetarian, and millions of people in the UK manage to do just that. Being a parent is difficult. Being the parent of an autistic child is different and very difficult. Please believe me, following this diet is not difficult. Thousands of people around the world manage to cope very well with the gf/cf diet. You can too.

The only difficult thing about this diet is deciding to do it. Everything else is straightforward.

Remember too, that this diet has very special rewards. A few weeks into it, you will notice the positive changes in your child. You will also be getting some extra sleep (sleep deprivation is a well-known and well-used torture technique). With the extra sleep and your child's improvements, life becomes less chaotic and stressful. A few weeks into the diet and you will feel far more able to cope.

I hope you are now convinced that the diet is not beyond your abilities, so on to the next big problem.

The diet is very expensive

It can be, but...

If you are determined never to cook, then yes, the diet will be expensive.

If you believe that your child's eating habits are not going to be affected (for the better!) by the diet, then I can understand why you would believe that the diet is going to be expensive.

The only example I can give you is the only one I can talk about with any confidence, which is my experience with Jack.

Pre-diet, Jack self-limited his food intake. He would only eat food that was predominantly stuffed to the hilt with gluten, casein or MSG. In fact, given his age, he was supremely clever at discovering food items which had two or even all three items in them, and refusing to eat anything else. It seemed (in retrospect), that his entire life was spent getting his next opiate 'fix'. As his body adjusted to the ever-increasing doses he was getting (and that I, in my ignorance, was only too happy to supply), he would then need even more of the opiates to maintain his needs/ addiction. Over the months and years, I had got into the habit of 'calming him down' (in reality giving him his next, much needed 'fix') every time he threw one of his violent wobblers/tantrums (which I now know were the result of him going through yet another 'withdrawal'), with milk and/or biscuits. He'd wake screaming and self-harming at night, and I'd give him milk. He'd wake after a nap and he'd get biscuits and juice (sugar free, and so it contained aspartame). If he didn't, he'd throw another of his wobblers. And so the day and night would go on. It was a vicious circle, but one I couldn't see at the time (I was far too tired and worn down).

I know this is all very interesting, but what has it got to do with the cost of the diet?

Well, if on the diet Jack was continuing to consume exactly the same type and amount of food and drink that he had pre-diet (only now it was the acceptable gf/cf substitutes), it is unlikely that I could afford to continue the diet long term without making some very unpleasant economic cutbacks. Luckily for all concerned, Jack's eating/drinking habits changed dramatically and very quickly.

Before the diet, Jack would happily consume, on a daily basis, three to four pints of milk, two to three yoghurts (or if he had fromage frais, he'd eat two to three pots at a sitting, they are such small pots!), a minimum of ten custard creams (two of these at a time, with a cup of milk, I had found to be the easiest and quickest way to put an end to a violent episode), a couple of packets of cheese and onion crisps (the poor boy always seemed so hungry!) and two soft white rolls (nothing on them, he liked to eat just the roll). All of this was on top of three meals a day. He was also drinking a cup of squash every 20–30 minutes. It was sugar free squash, because I was being a conscientious mum, concerned about dental decay in her children. I just need to point out here that I didn't find out about the effects of aspartame and take it out of Jack's diet until he'd been on the diet for eight months. So even on the diet he was drinking nearly as much squash. He'd really clamour for it. Since I've taken aspartame out of his diet, he rarely asks for a drink (he couldn't possibly have been addicted to the stuff, could he?!). I now have to remember to give him enough liquid every day.

Adding that up for you, in the prices of 2000, Jack was eating/drinking approximately £3.50 a day (£24.50 a week) *on top of his three meals.* If he had continued to eat and drink like this, but consuming gf/cf substitutes (shop bought, not home made), the cost would have been approximately £7.60 a day (£53.40 a week), before he'd even eaten his three meals a day. Who can afford that? I can see the car being sold and the telephone being unplugged for starters.

Would you believe me if I said that Jack's entire daily intake of food and drink (main meals included), does not even come close to the original £3.50 a day that he used to get through just in snacks? Please believe me, because I have just spent a very unpleasant 30 minutes totting up Jack's daily diet and costing it out. And spare a thought for my poor milkman who saw his profits drop substantially when Jack went on the diet.

That isn't to say that some of the basics of a gf/cf diet are not expensive. They are. The cost of gf/cf bread is disgraceful. It doesn't matter if you make it yourself (it's cheaper, but not cheap) or buy it ready-made, it is still very expensive. But Jack now eats very little bread (why should he eat as much, when he's not getting 'high' on it any more?). Jack and I are also fortunate in that we have a very supportive GP, who provides some of Jack's bread on NHS prescription (more about that later). He now only gets custard creams at his nursery and only because all the other children get biscuits at break time. I'm very grateful that Jack no longer lives for eating custard creams, as the gf/cf versions are incredibly expensive. He just doesn't ask for them any more. He has a gf/cf yoghurt or similar for dessert, once a day. Crisps are now a rarity in his diet. He doesn't scream for them any more. Mind you, it took me a long time to readjust to Jack's new eating habits. For many months, I was cramming the poor child with gf/cf substitutes for the snacks he previously 'enjoyed'. It slowly dawned on me that if he wasn't asking for it, he probably didn't want it (need it) any more. Now, Jack eats three meals a day and very occasionally a snack.

The vast majority of food for this diet is available at your supermarket. It is just 'normal' food. Fresh meat, fish, vegetables, fruit and rice are fine for the gf/cf diet. Other gf/cf foods – sauces, packet mixes, convenience foods, etc. – are available at the supermarkets; much of what you already buy may be fine or you may have to switch brands. There are only a few foods or ingredients that you will have either to buy from specialist suppliers or make for yourself.

In conclusion, it is safest to say that initially you will find the diet expensive; but as your child readjusts his eating habits, you will find that the diet gets cheaper and cheaper, until it reaches an acceptable level. If your child's eating habits are similar to Jack's pre-diet eating patterns, then, I hope, you too will be quids in on the diet.

Is it necessary to remove gluten, casein, MSG and aspartame from my child's diet? Won't I get results by removing just one of them?

Usually the question is phrased along the lines of, 'I can handle taking milk out of my child's diet but removing gluten seems far too difficult'. MSG and aspartame tend to get overlooked!

Many parents report that they see startling improvements when they remove casein from their child's diet. In fact these changes can be so amazing that the parent does not feel that there will be any further benefit to be gained by going on to remove gluten, MSG and aspartame. If you feel yourself falling into this trap, please go back and read the chapter on the opioid excess theory. If your child benefits from removing one of these items from their diet, then you *must* remove the others. Gluten and casein are so very similar in their chemical make-up, that if your child is producing peptides from one of these proteins, then they will also be producing peptides from the other. Lots of medical research backs up this statement (see Further Reading at the back of the book), and as for MSG and aspartame, I hope the chapter devoted to those two nasties has convinced you that they are not good for anyone.

If you only remove one of these opiates from your child's diet you may notice a startling change in your child. But this is unlikely to remain the situation for very long. One of two things will happen.

First, if you use the drug addict analogy, all you have done by removing either casein or gluten from your child's diet is reduce your child's intake of the opiates. They are still getting a 'fix' from the remaining opiate. Their body will eventually readjust to this lower level and you will notice that the startling changes that have already occurred, far from increasing or even levelling off, will begin to disappear and your child will slowly revert back to how they were before you began the diet.

The second scenario is that your child will notice that you are depriving them of the 'fix' that they are used to and will make up the difference by increasing their levels of gluten-containing foods. Again, you will be back to where you started. If your child is clever enough to work out which foods give them the level of gluten-based opiates they need, you may well never see an improvement at all when you take them off casein. They will almost immediately begin to compensate by eating more gluten-containing foods. It is quite likely you will despair of the diet working for your child and throw in the towel.

The final thing I have to say in answering this question is me being brutally honest. If your child benefits from the removal of either gluten or casein from their diet, then you know that your child has an opiate/peptide/intolerance problem. If your child produces peptides from either gluten or casein, they will be producing peptides from the other. You now know the effect that these peptides have been having upon your child. No one deliberately sets out to harm their child or deliberately to feed them poison, but if you remove either gluten or casein from your child's diet and do not remove the other, that is exactly what you are doing – harming your child by allowing them to continue to consume something which is poisoning them. OK, lecture over, on to the next question.

How strict do you have to be?

The answer in a nutshell is very, very strict. This is an all or nothing diet. It is not like a calorie control diet: you can't give your child 'sinful' food as an occasional treat. Not only would you be guilty of poisoning your child (see above), but you would also be undoing all of the good work you have already done in getting the gluten and casein out of your child's system. Introducing a forbidden food will only start your child craving gluten and casein opiates all over again. So when you start the diet, that's it. No more casein or gluten ever again.

I don't think my child has food allergies *or* My child doesn't restrict their food intake to gluten and casein foods – will they still benefit from the diet?

Two separate questions that are in essence covering the same point: *How do I know if this diet will help my child?*

I appreciate that this wasn't a question I needed to answer with Jack. His food intake was totally restricted to foods that had gluten and casein in them. That he had also found foods that combined these two with MSG and aspartame was purely a bonus as far as he was concerned.

Please remember that although those following this diet are usually said to have a food allergy or intolerance, and that even the best organisation to help you is called Allergy induced Autism (AiA), your child isn't suffering from a true allergy. They are suffering from an inability to break down two proteins and cope with digesting other foods. If only these children would break out in spots or hives when they ate gluten or casein, how much easier life would be for all of us. Their reactions to these foods are far more complex and therefore so much harder to pinpoint. It is only when you have removed the offending items from their diet that you will begin to get a clear idea of what they were doing to your child. It very often depends on how your child's autism manifests itself, as to how the effects of the peptides show themselves. In truth, it is just easier to call this problem an allergy or an intolerance, than to go down the road of long-winded explanations of peptides and opiates with someone who really doesn't want to know.

My guess is that if your child is not restricting themselves to a predominantly gluten and casein diet, they will fall into one of the two following categories.

The first is the child who seems to have a very good appetite. Too good, in fact. So good is their appetite that they eat everything that is put in front of them. They are getting a good, balanced diet. You have absolutely no concerns about their diet. Well, perhaps they always seem hungry. They may have eaten a huge meal; they may well have even tried to eat part of yours as well. You could often give them a snack straight away after a meal and they'd wolf it down as if they had not eaten. If this description fits your child, then it may well be the case that they have come to recognise that food is 'good'. Or rather, it makes them feel good (an opiate high). They just haven't worked out which of the foods it is that they eat that makes them feel good. So they work on the principle that if they eat enough food, it will give them that 'good' feeling. Sooner or later, they will have eaten enough gluten and casein from a normal, well-balanced diet to get all the opiates that they require.

Or perhaps you have a child who barely eats anything. Their food intake or lack of it is a constant source of anxiety. They don't appear to be eating enough to stay alive. They seem to get by on the smallest amount of food or go long periods of time without eating. This child has worked out that food makes them feel 'bad'. After the 'high' of a gluten/casein 'fix', they know they are going to feel very, very bad – the withdrawal period. They haven't worked out which foods it is that make them feel bad, so the poor things do their very best to avoid all foods for as long as possible.

If your child fits either of the two descriptions above, then yes, they will benefit from the diet, just as much as a child like Jack, who restricted his food intake to predominantly gluten and casein.

But at the end of the day, does it really matter if your child does or doesn't fall into a category? Give the diet a go. What have you got to lose? Just four weeks. That is all it is going to take to 'prove' if the diet will work for your child. Surely we can all spare 28 days out of our lives to try to make a difference to our children!

If this still doesn't convince you (help! What more do I have to write to convince you it is worth trying?), you can always go the traditional science/medical route and get concrete proof before you proceed with the diet. There is a centre in the UK which will test a sample of your child's urine to see if it contains the peptides which originate from gluten and casein. The details of the Autism Research Unit are to be found in the Directory of Useful Contacts at the back of the book.

I in no way wish to devalue the very important work that the Autism Research Unit are doing in this field, but my personal opinion is that the evidence before your eyes (the changes in your child, once they are on the diet), is overwhelming and far outweighs any scientific evidence that can be offered.

But the test results from the Autism Research Unit are a very powerful thing to possess. Even if you do not need the test results to convince you that the diet is worth a try, it is a wonderful piece of paper to wave in front of sceptical partners, relatives, health professionals, teachers, etc. The Autism Research Unit is one of only three centres in the world (and the only one in the UK) which are able to do this test. Both the Autism Research Unit and the person in charge, Paul Shattock, are highly regarded around the world and there are few people prepared to argue with these test results.

Help! My child only eats foods that have gluten and casein in them *or* My child already restricts his own diet. I don't think I can cope with restricting it further. What can I do? He will starve!

This is a real dilemma and one that I can strongly sympathise with, through my own experiences with Jack. On the one hand you know that what your child is eating is hurting/harming them, but you also know from painful and frustrating experience that your child is adamant about what they will and will not eat. Heaven knows, in the past you've done everything you could think of to extend their diet and it has failed miserably. They eat the same foods day in and day out. Their range of 'acceptable' foods is tiny. When you go out, you have to remember to pack a bag full of meals, snacks and drinks which you know they will eat. You may even have the added problem that your child is brand-specific in their choice of foods.

Right now, it is understandable that you are panicking. They already restrict their diet and now you plan to restrict it further. In all likelihood that restriction will mean taking out of their diet all, or nearly all, of the foods that they eat. The way it is looking at the moment, your child is highly likely to starve. Please try not to worry; your child is highly unlikely to starve itself. Learn from one of my many mistakes in implementing the diet and substitute gf/cf foods for the foods that they are already happy to eat. Despite the previous experiences you may have had with your child, it will work.

Confession time: Jack did not eat a single food that did not contain either gluten or casein. To put Jack on the diet meant that I had to take out everything that he was willing to eat and replace it with gf/cf food. When Jack started the diet, he had been eating the same type of foods for 18 months. Every time I had tried to introduce a new food, Jack either threw the mother of all temper tantrums or refused to eat. If I physically put new food in his mouth (what a struggle), he'd either spit it out straight away or he would just keep it in his mouth until out of sheer frustration I'd either get him to spit it out or I'd have manually to take it out of his mouth. This is just to illustrate that he would not eat anything he didn't want to. For the six months prior to the diet he'd eaten the same thing for breakfast every day (toast), he'd had the same thing for lunch every day (burger, bread roll, chips and at least one yoghurt) and the same thing for dinner every day (chicken flavoured noodles – brand specific – and yet more yoghurt) and during the day he would snack on bread, biscuits, cake and crisps. OK, I realised he wasn't getting a balanced diet, but at least the three-plus pints of milk he was drinking a day were good for him (how wrong can you be?). Looking on the bright side, it made shopping and cooking straight-forward (and very repetitive). Is it any wonder that I kept putting the diet off?

Jack, you will be pleased to know, didn't starve. On his fourth birthday (six months into the diet), he was wearing clothes made for a six-year-old. He is thriving. That isn't to say he now eats a wide, varied and balanced diet. He doesn't. He still restricts the foods that he is prepared to eat. But now, not only are the foods that he is eating not damaging him, but he is also eating a far wider range of foods than he did before the diet. He will now occasionally ask to try a new food. Sometimes we strike it lucky and he will continue to eat this new food.

I've already admitted that I made the big mistake of supplementing his diet during the first week with Hula Hoops, which contain MSG. Even if you have to supplement your child's food intake during the first awkward days of the diet with what would normally be an unacceptable amount of gf/cf crisps/chips/biscuits etc., it will not hurt them in the short term. If your child is currently only eating gluten- and casein-based foods, then I suspect that the last thing they are getting at the moment is a balanced diet.

If you feel that you and your child fit this description, then the best thing you can possibly do is give yourself some extra time to prepare before implementing the diet. You will be able to offer your child gf/cf replacements for all the food he currently eats, but you may need to spend a little time finding or making the food. You can do this and your child will not starve. You may have an awkward few days (I will cover this later), but your child will not starve. Once he is on the diet, all your fears and anxieties will be a thing of the past and you really will reap the rewards of having put them to one side so that you could implement the diet.

It is a good idea for you to get your child a good vitamin and mineral supplement. If nothing else, it will probably go a long way to giving you some peace of mind. I felt a whole lot better once I started giving Jack a good supplement daily. There is a list of very good suppliers in the Specialist Suppliers section at the back of the book. If you are going to use a supplement that can be purchased from a chemist or supermarket, please contact the manufacturers before giving it to your child, to ensure that it does not contain gluten or casein.

How do I know that any improvements in my child are due to the diet and not just to do with a natural improvement due to his age and/or other treatments?

This is a question posed by the die-hard sceptics.

First of all, it is a good idea when embarking on the diet to keep a diary of your child's behaviour, language, sleep patterns and toileting, before the diet and when they are on the diet. That way you will be able to 'see' just how well the diet is working.

It is very easy to overlook the small changes that are occurring, when there are far more startling ones happening at the same time. The diary will serve you well in the future, when you come across people who don't believe that the diet can possibly make any difference. A written diary is often seen as more 'concrete' proof than listening to what some might call parental anecdotes. Also it is very easy, after some months on the diet, to forget just what your child was like prior to the diet. Hindsight is a wonderful thing, but it is rarely reliable.

Remember that this diet is not meant to be a stand-alone treatment for your child. It is not a substitute for traditional help such as speech, physio and occupational therapy. The diet should work in harmony with these approaches. It is obvious that if your child is on the diet and feeling well, they will benefit far more from such help than if they are locked into a continuous cycle of opiate-induced highs and lows.

Isn't the calcium in milk necessary for my child's health?

By now, you will have realised the effect that milk is having upon your child's health. It isn't good.

But calcium is required by the human body and we all know that animal milk is a good source of calcium. We are always being encouraged to drink milk daily and in the UK it is deemed such an important food that if a family is on Income Support and has a child under the age of five years, they are given tokens that can be exchanged for full fat milk. So what can you do?

It's time to explode some myths and get my name taken off the Milk Marketing Board's Christmas card list.

- Four-fifths of the world's population are allergic to milk. The majority of these people are allergic to lactose (milk sugar), as they do not produce the enzyme necessary to digest it. If milk was the only good source of calcium then most of the world have a problem. They don't.

- Milk intolerance is the commonest food intolerance in the under fives.

- Removal of dairy products from the diet is common in the treatment of allergies such as eczema and asthma.

- There are far better sources of calcium than milk. Broccoli and most green-leaf vegetables are a better source of calcium than milk. Calcium can be found in numerous other foods: soya beans/tofu, almonds, brazil nuts, sesame seeds, carrots, garlic, cauliflower, rhubarb and beans – the list goes on and on.

- If you do not have a hope of getting your child to eat any of the calcium-containing foods listed above (join the club!), there are plenty of very good calcium supplements available.

- Lots of foods have calcium added to them, e.g. breakfast cereals, soya-based milks and yoghurts.

- The majority of dairy-based foods are high in saturated fats. These fats have been linked to heart disease and various cancers.

- Cows are routinely fed antibiotics and scientific studies have found that these antibiotics (designed for cows) are in the milk we drink.

- Further research has shown that a hormone present in cow's milk can block the absorption of calcium by humans.

- At the end of the day, cow's milk is designed by nature for baby cows. All animal milk is very different in structure from human milk, which is the only milk designed to be consumed by us and then only by babies and infants.

The heavy promotion of milk as a healthy and necessary part of the human diet is a relatively new concept, only a few decades old, and it is a testament to a clever marketing campaign that we all believe it. That the vast majority of the world's population is unable to tolerate milk means that it is a substance that the human body was never designed to consume. That our children have a problem with it too (for different reasons), only means that they are in the majority.

There are lots and lots of really good books (far too many to mention here) on the subject of milk intolerances and many more filled with recipes. A quick browse in any good bookshop will provide you with all that you may need on the subject.

How long will it be before I see the results of the diet? *or*
How long do I continue with the diet before giving it up?

Most parents have reported that they start noticing improvements in their child within a few days of removing milk from the diet. Urine tests have shown that the milk peptides leave the body within three days. Gluten peptides unfortunately take a lot longer and it can be several months before they have removed themselves from your child's body.

Go back and read the section covering the necessity of removing both gluten and casein from your child's diet. You will now appreciate that once you have successfully removed all milk and milk-related substances from your child's diet, you cannot afford to rest on your laurels. Instead you must begin immediately to remove gluten, MSG and aspartame from your child's diet. If you don't, your child's body will begin to readjust to the smaller amounts of opiates available to it and all the progress that your child has made will begin to be lost.

Do not be surprised if when you remove the very last source of peptides, your child appears to get worse/regress to how they were before the diet began/exhibit behaviours that they never had before. These are all very short-term problems and are caused by your child's withdrawal from the peptides. They will be over in a few days at the very most. Try not to look at this temporary development in your child as an alarming and permanent problem. See it instead as a justification and validation that the diet is going to help your child. If your child didn't have a problem with gluten and casein, they wouldn't be having withdrawal symptoms. Withdrawal means there is a problem and you are solving the problem, by putting your child on the diet.

So, you should begin to see the positive effects of the diet upon your child very quickly. As long as you continue to implement the diet by removing other offending items, the progress of your child will continue.

There are two things that you need to bear in mind when you are trying to assess the benefits of the diet and the speed of the improvements in your child. The first is that although your child's diet is now gf/cf, their body won't be gf/cf for some while, as it will take time for the offending peptides to get out of their body. The second point is that the damage that gluten and casein did to your child did not happen overnight and therefore it is unrealistic to expect the developmental delays they caused to disappear immediately. What removing gluten and casein from your child's diet will do, is prevent any more damage occurring and create a situation which will allow your child to catch up. The younger your child is when you get them on the gf/cf diet, the quicker you will see the results, as the developmental delays that have occurred are of a shorter duration. For example, if your child is three years old when they start the diet, they can only have a maximum developmental delay of three years (in practice it will be far less). If your child is eight years old when they start the diet, the maximum developmental delay they can have experienced is eight years – that is an awful lot of catching up to do compared to the three-year-old. It really isn't realistic to expect every child to follow the same patterns of improvement on the diet. But every child will improve.

If you do not see any benefits at all (however small), within two weeks of the diet (that is, having taken all the gluten, casein, MSG and aspartame out of your child's diet), then you will have to look very carefully at what your child is doing to get the forbidden opiates. It may well be (and it is often the case), that gluten or casein is still managing to sneak into the diet. Go through the ingredients of the foods you are feeding them again, just to make sure you haven't overlooked a potential source of gluten and casein or that the manufacturer hasn't changed the ingredients since you first checked them. This unfortunately does happen occasionally and it is always wise to be on your guard and periodically check the ingredients.

Alternatively, your child may be getting the opiates when they are out of your control. Are they sharing food at playgroup or school? Jack was once given some sweets by the child sitting next to him on the school bus. It was lucky for Jack that these sweets were gf/cf. Or else they could be getting gluten or casein from a non-food source, such as play dough. Both commercial and home-made play dough contain a very high level of gluten. There is a recipe for gf/cf play dough in the recipe section of the book that is very easy and cheap to make. Jack not only managed to get gluten from some home-made play dough at his playgroup but also discovered that dried rabbit food was a great source of gluten and so he became very friendly with our rabbit for a couple of days, until I discovered what he was doing. Now the rabbit food is kept well out of his way. All dried pet food, including fish food and dog biscuits, is a source of gluten.

Contamination of your child's food by gluten and casein can easily happen when you are storing, preparing and cooking it. I will cover this in great depth later. You may also notice for the first few days of the diet that your child develops some unusual scavenging habits. Jack spent his first week with one or both hands down the back of the sofa, scavenging for food crumbs. He also paid a great deal of attention to the carpet, especially the bits I didn't usually vacuum (under the sofa and right up to the skirting board – I've already admitted to being a housework failure), in his search for biscuit crumbs. And I'm surprised that poor Luke didn't develop a complex about eating, as I used to hover around him when he was eating and swoop on any stray crumbs that he produced when he ate biscuits/sandwiches/toast, etc. For a while the vacuum seemed never to be unplugged and I did start to vacuum under the sofa, along the skirting boards and down the back of all the chairs. This behaviour of Jack's didn't last long, but if I hadn't realised what he was doing and taken such drastic measures (vacuuming is a drastic measure in my book), he would have continued to consume gluten and casein long after I thought he had stopped. I would have been looking for improvements when none would have been possible, as he would have been still producing peptides and they would in turn have been producing the damaging opiates. I could have easily given up on the diet, believing it wasn't working. The moral of this story is never to underestimate how devious your child will become in trying to seek out new sources for his 'fix'.

Will I need to do two weekly shopping trips – one at the health food store, for my child on the diet, and one at the supermarket for the rest of the family?

No, you won't!

I go to the health food store once every four to six weeks, to stock up on the gf/cf biscuits that Jack takes in to the nursery and to buy some gf/cf vanilla puddings he and Luke are very fond of. Very occasionally, I buy gf/cf ice cream. I prefer to make the boys ice cream and I could easily make the puddings, but they are a good standby for those days when any attempt at sticking to a routine proves impossible. And I could never, ever make custard creams look like shop-bought ones. The only other things that I buy especially for Jack are gf flours and xanthan gum, which I order by phone from Barbara's Kitchen (number in Specialist Suppliers Directory). His bread I get on prescription via my local chemist. Very occasionally, I order gf/cf packet bakery mixes, via the phone, to act as a standby for those days when I either don't have the time or the inclination to bake cakes, etc. Everything else, I get from my local supermarket. You really will be surprised at the amount of food that is available at your supermarket that is gf/cf.

I knew you wouldn't believe me, so I spent a very boring couple of evenings doing a little research to prove it to you. I chose two supermarkets at random, Tesco and Sainsbury, and decided to find out how many gf/cf food items they stock. Please bear in mind:

- The food listed may well contain food that has MSG/aspartame in it. Neither store produces a list for foods free of MSG/aspartame (sorry, but I wasn't prepared to spend the following two weeks trapped in supermarkets, finding out which of the items had MSG/aspartame in them).

- The food only refers to the store's own-brand products.

- The lists excludes: fresh, frozen and cooked meat and fish, fresh vegetables and fruit and all fruit juices – all of which are acceptable on the gf/cf diet (check cooked meat and fish to ensure that nothing has been added during the cooking process that would render it unsuitable for the diet). The list also excludes teas and coffees.

Sainsbury declare that all the following of their own brand are gf/cf:

- all soft drinks – carbonated (in cans), dilutables, mixers, UHT fruit juices, water and flavoured waters. Although I would imagine that a fair amount of these would contain aspartame

- all lards, drippings and cooking oils

- all canned fish in oil or brine

- all canned fruit

- all vinegars

- all seasonings

- all jams, conserves, honey and fruit spreads
- all plain frozen vegetables
- all plain canned vegetables in salt water and sugar water.

On top of that lot, they do another 335 own-brand items that are gf/cf. This includes seven types of sausages, four breakfast cereals, 14 types of sweets, three sorbets, five different ice lollies, six preprepared chilled foods, two frozen prepared meals and 26 ready-made sauces or sauce mixes.

Tesco have 1162 own-brand items that are gf/cf (plus some meats that are either prepacked or on their deli counter – sorry, but I got bored of cross-checking and counting these). These include six breakfast cereals, three ice cream sauces, four ice lollies, 23 different types of sweets and one sausage variety.

If that is just the supermarket own brands, it will give an idea of the range and scope of foods that are available to you at your supermarket.

The only extra shopping you need to do can usually be done via the phone and all you need for that is a credit or debit card. The Specialist Suppliers and Mail Order Directory at the back of the book will let you know what is available and where you can purchase the items you require.

What about genetically modified food?

This isn't a question I have ever been asked by a parent (yet), but it is as good a place as any to deal with it here.

GM food may well be the miracle food we've all been waiting for, enabling countries to grow enough food to feed their populations. Technically, it will even be possible to produce gluten free cereals.

The problem that GM food can pose for our children on the gf/cf diet is that there are, as yet, no long-term studies on the effects to human health from consuming GM food and there are unlikely to be any for a considerable amount of time. There may well be no side effects or risks. But our children are more likely to eat a disproportionately high amount of food which contains GM ingredients compared to the rest of the population. This is especially the case because much soya and corn that is currently grown in the US is GM. If there are side effects from this food, then it goes without saying that our children are more likely to develop them. It is possible and very easy to get soya-based food/milk that does not contain GM soya. One of the major producers of gf/cf soya-based foods, Provamel, are currently guaranteeing that all of their soya is derived from a non-GM source. Many of the other specialist food suppliers also produce gf/cf food which is free from GM ingredients. Because of the current controversy over the possible effects of GM food, many food manufacturers and supermarkets are labelling foods which are GM free.

As with so much else in life, the decision is yours.

Beware of the Internet, *or* international 'Chinese Whispers'

The Internet is a wonderful thing. It is like having the world's biggest library at your disposal. Better still, the 'book' you desperately want is never going to be booked out to someone else; everything is always available to you. Not only will you be able to find suppliers of the foods that you want and chase up the latest scientific research, there are also some really great websites on the gf/cf diet for autistic children (see Directory of Useful Contacts for some of the better ones), and the information they carry and update regularly can be invaluable.

They can also be an absolute nightmare. There have been several incidents where a problem with cross-contamination, on a local or national scale, has thrown parents across the world into an unnecessary panic.

There are two examples that illustrate this point well. The first was when a parent suspected that the buckwheat flour (a gf flour) she was using was causing an allergic reaction in her son. So concerned was she, that she sent a sample of it off to be analysed at a laboratory. The test results came back and confirmed her fears; there was gluten present in the buckwheat. This information duly got posted on a gf/cf website and caused panic on both sides of the Atlantic. Parents stopped buying buckwheat flour and anything that contained buckwheat. A bit of snooping into this problem and all was resolved. A particular consignment of buckwheat flour had got contaminated by a gluten-containing flour. What was a very small-scale, localised, problem in the US became, in an international game of Chinese Whispers, a worldwide disaster. Suddenly it seemed as if the world stocks of buckwheat were contaminated with gluten and this had major repercussions around the world.

The other example was when one parent replied to a question posted at a website about the practices of a very well-known international fast-food company. The parent who was answering the question had worked for the company when she had been a student, and based her answers on her experience at that time. The answers were not favourable to the company and many parents boycotted the company's outlets. It caused some parents in Britain to do the same. But there were two fundamental problems with this. One was that the information could well have been out of date. Companies change their practices and procedures many times over the years. What may well have caused a problem in our children ten years or even one year ago could have been changed, to the benefit of our children. The second problem was that parents presumed that the practices of the company were the same in both America and Britain. They may well have been but in this case they were not, and the company concerned had very different policies in the UK – ones that meant some of their products were suitable for inclusion on the diet.

So by all means, surf the Net for information and advice. It can be absolutely invaluable. But treat what you find there with caution. There really is no substitute for checking information yourself and basing your decisions on the correct information.

Other contentious issues

Periodically the same story does the rounds: there is gluten and/or casein in toothpaste, soap powder, detergent, dishwasher powder and postage stamps. All major manufacturers have been contacted and there is no truth to these rumours. Of course it doesn't do any harm to contact the manufacturer yourself to be sure. But unless your child develops a reaction to any of the above (if they do, it is more likely that they are allergic to another ingredient in the product), I wouldn't worry about it.

Starting the Diet

You are now determined to start implementing the diet with your child. In fact you are raring to go, but before you begin removing all the gluten, casein, etc. from your child's diet there are a few things that it is wise to do first. In the short term, they may prevent you from implementing the diet for a week or two, but in the long term they will save you time and tears.

Get some medical support

The first thing that you will need to do is to make an appointment to see both your child's GP and paediatrician. Explain to them the theory behind the diet, if they are not aware of it (most paediatricians are, but not many GPs will be) and that you wish to implement the diet for a trial period of three months, to see if it has any beneficial effect upon your child. Although you will see improvements in your child in much less than three months, it will give you a little extra leeway. Ask if an appointment can be made with a dietician to check that your child's diet, when they are gf/cf, is not lacking anything essential to their long-term health.

Whilst you are waiting for these appointments to come through, contact the Autism Research Unit (details in Directory of Useful Contacts), to arrange for a urine test to be carried out, to see if/prove that gluten and casein opioids are present in your child. Having a piece of medical evidence that backs up what you are doing is always handy, especially if you have a sceptical partner (most of us do, in the beginning!), doctor, relative, etc. However, be warned: because the Autism Research Unit is one of only three centres in the world that offer this service, it can take some time to get the results back.

Since this waiting time can be frustrating, especially if you are ready to get started on the diet, there is nothing to prevent you from sending off your child's urine sample and then implementing the diet before getting the results back, which is what many parents do. If this is the course you are planning to take, please check that the Autism Research Unit has received the sample before you remove gluten and casein from your child's diet. Of course if you are the one sceptical about the diet, then you will want to have the test results back before you consider starting the diet.

A word of warning

Before you see anyone about this diet, you will need to be positive in your own mind that the diet is something that you wish to do, to help your child. Although most of the parents who are following this diet with their child are fortunate enough to have the backing of their GP and paediatrician, there are parents who come across either disbelief or stiff opposition to the diet, from the medical community. Sometimes these attitudes can undermine the confidence of the parent to such an extent that they will either delay the implementation of the diet or believe what they hear from these medical sceptics, write the whole thing off as a silly idea and never attempt the diet.

Prepare yourself

The next and by far the most important thing you need to do is to prepare yourself before beginning the diet. How you prepare for implementing the diet will be largely dictated by your own personality and your child's age and eating habits. But please, if you suffer from the 'bull in the china shop' mentality that I do, try to rein it in for a few weeks. It really will save you time and effort in the long run. The following pointers may well help you.

You will need to look closely at what your child is currently eating

There is no point in trying to introduce gf/cf foods that are completely alien to your child; you will just be making life unnecessarily difficult for yourself and your child. You've probably tried very hard in the past to introduce new foods to your child, with varying degrees of success (or complete failure, which was always the case with Jack). When you are removing gluten and casein from your child's diet (in effect depriving them of something they need, want or are craving), your child just isn't going to be in the mood to try new foods. If you try to get them to eat food that is alien to their diet, you will merely end up with a hungry and very unhappy child and a bin full of uneaten food, and you will be feeling, at the very least, frustrated. This book is all about making life as easy as possible, so instead, list the foods that your child is currently willing to eat and set about finding their gf/cf alternatives.

If your child currently eats a wide variety of foods, finding gf/cf alternatives will not cause you much of a problem. You will find that much of what they are already eating is acceptable for the diet. Apart from finding suitable replacements for items such as bread, biscuits and cakes, you will just need to make a few minor adjustments to their main meals, i.e. mashing their potatoes with a gf/cf margarine, substituting a gf/cf gravy, serving gf/cf pasta.

If your child already limits the foods that they eat, you will find this process a little harder, but it is not impossible. There are gf/cf alternatives for just about everything. Sausages, tinned spaghetti, burgers, pizza, pasta, chips, crisps, yoghurt and ice cream – you name it, you should be able to find a suitable alternative. The only things I haven't been able to find a gf/cf alternative for yet are chicken nuggets, fish fingers and gravy, but they are very easy to make.

Check the Specialist Suppliers Directory at the end of the book to find out who is making what and where you can get hold of what you need. Don't forget that your supermarket also carries a lot of gf/cf food as part of its own-brand range and much that is made by the large food manufacturers is also gf/cf.

Also look in the gf/cf recipe section and have a go at making what you need. As someone who rarely went into the kitchen, except to turn the kettle on or take something out of the microwave, it is immensely satisfying to see your child eat something that you've taken some time preparing. Of course the reverse is also true – it is heartbreaking having something that you have cooked rejected (a polite way of putting it) by your child. It is for this reason if for no other that you should initially stick to providing only gf/cf foods that replace something that your child is already happy to eat.

So you've now seen all those people whom you need to see within the medical profession, your cupboards and fridge/freezer are bulging at the seams with gf/cf foods for your child, what do you do next?

Decide how you wish to approach the diet

There are only two ways of implementing the diet. One way is to remove all gluten, casein, MSG and aspartame in one go. The other way is to stagger the removal of the foods, one at a time.

If you are implementing the diet with a pre-school aged child (and these seem to be in the majority at the moment), you can probably, just about, get away with removing everything from your child's diet in one go.

If you have a school aged child or teenager or are preparing the diet for an adult, then I would strongly recommend not withdrawing gluten and casein at the same time. There are many reasons for this, but the primary one is that if your child or an adult has strong withdrawal symptoms from the removal of gluten and casein (and remember that they are addicted to these substances, so they will be in effect going 'cold turkey'), I for one would not like to be around to witness this or to have to try to control them or keep them safe.

Of course it goes without saying that if you withdraw all the offending foods in one go, you will see improvements in your child faster and you will only have to make one set of adjustments regarding shopping and cooking. If you are keen and eager to get going, you may well think that this is the right way to go. But this diet is all about helping your child and this book is about making the process of implementing the diet as pain free and stress free as possible. Your child going cold turkey will not help them, nor will it leave you stress free.

I have already admitted elsewhere in this book that I made Jack go cold turkey. I have also admitted that this was not the best thing I could have done. In my defence, it was done in ignorance. Yes, Jack and I did cope with it, but Jack was three and a half years old and so I could physically handle him and keep him and me relatively safe.

Most parents prefer to remove casein rather than gluten from their child's diet first. This is because they feel that removing milk products from their child's diet is easier than removing gluten. If you are still unsure that the diet will work for your child, then removing casein from the diet is a good way to see if there are any improvements noticeable in your child (I'm sure by now I do not have to say this, but just in case – remember that you will not see the full benefits until gluten, aspartame and MSG are removed too).

MSG and aspartame are fairly easy to remove from the diet. If you are going to stagger the removal of foods from your child's diet, it is usually easier to remove MSG and aspartame at the same time as you remove gluten, for they are primarily found in soft drinks and gluten-containing foods.

When you remove casein from your child's diet, there are two points you will need to bear in mind. The first is that in removing casein from the diet, you will also by necessity be removing some gluten. Many processed foods that contain casein will also contain gluten (and MSG and aspartame). The second and most important point is that you will need to set yourself a date for removing the gluten, MSG and aspartame as well. Remember that if you leave too long a gap between removing casein and then gluten, your child's body will readjust to the new lower level of opiates it is receiving and you will see all the good that has occurred from removing casein from your child's diet beginning to be undone (see Misconceptions and Commonly Asked Questions – 'Is it necessary to remove gluten, casein, MSG and aspartame from my child's diet?' for a fuller explanation).

Informing others

You will need to let everyone who shares the responsibility of looking after your child (grandparents, teachers, nursery staff, childminders, baby sitters, etc.) know what you are doing. Explain to them fully what you are doing and why you are doing it. Supply them with gf/cf alternatives, give them a list of the forbidden foods, enlist their help and ask them to report back to you any improvements that they notice in your child.

Replacing milk with soya milk in your child's diet

As soya milk is the easiest milk alternative to obtain, it is likely that you will select this as a replacement for milk in your child's diet. Check the ingredients of the brand carefully, as flavoured and sweetened varieties of soya milk can sometimes contain gluten.

Soya milk has quite a strong and different flavour compared to cow's milk and often a child offered a glass of it will reject it. One way that many parents have reported as successful in getting their child to drink soya milk is to take a gradual approach when introducing it. Try giving your child a cup of cow's milk as normal and just top it up with a tiny amount of soya milk (and I do mean a tiny amount). Each day, gradually increase the ratio of soya milk to cow's milk, until your child is drinking pure soya milk. Many of the parents who report that their child refuses to drink soya milk add that their child is happy to have soya milk with breakfast cereal. So this can be another way that your child can get used to the taste of soya milk. It really is worth taking the time to introduce soya milk to your child before you start the diet.

Trying to eliminate cross-contamination

The most common way that gluten or casein are going accidentally to sneak into your child's diet will be in your kitchen, either when you are preparing/cooking your child's food or in how/where you store it. The ways in which this can happen are almost endless, but I've listed below some of the most common mistakes that have been made by parents:

- Do not use the family toaster for toasting gf/cf bread. You will already know that you dare not move your toaster, for fear of the avalanche of breadcrumbs that will occur. Well, those same breadcrumbs are going to come into contact with your child's bread and by the time it pops out of the toaster, it will no longer be gf/cf. Either buy a separate toaster for gf/cf bread and make sure that everyone in the household knows which toaster is for which bread, or alternatively, toast the gf/cf bread under the grill, remembering of course to line the grill each time with a fresh piece of foil.

- Do not keep gf/cf bread in the bread bin, along with ordinary bread.

- Do not keep gf/cf biscuits in a biscuit tin, along with ordinary biscuits.

- Only use gf/cf margarine for gf/cf bread. Gluten from ordinary bread is easily transferred on a knife into the margarine.

- Keep the jar of jam/spread that your child uses separate from other jams/spreads. If necessary, keep two jars of the same jam/spread on the go, one for the gf/cf diet and another for the rest of the family. Make sure you mark the jars, so that everyone knows which is which. In this house, everything that is for Jack's use only is marked with a big blue cross, from a permanent marker pen.

- Do not use a deep fat fryer for cooking gf/cf food. If you do rely upon a deep fat fryer/chip pan a lot (chips and chicken nuggets seem always to be a favourite food) then either buy a second one, which will only be used for gf/cf food, or decide that the one you've got is only going to be used for gf/cf food in future. If you take the second choice, then you have to drain off the oil and replace it. You are also going to have to scrub the machine out, as if your life depended upon it, to remove all the many traces of gluten and casein that will be stuck to the inside, which have come from breadcrumbs and batters.

- Buy a sieve/colander that will only be used for gf/cf foods. I don't know about you, but my sieves never stand up to a close inspection; never mind how much I try to clean the things, something always seems reluctant to be shifted.

- Saucepans, frying pans, baking trays, sponge tins and loaf tins will always need to be thoroughly cleaned before being used with gf/cf food. That tiny speck of mashed potato/custard/gravy that always seems to be stuck on a pan, even though you can remember scouring the life out of it the last time you used it (please don't let me be the only one that this happens to!), will contaminate your child's food with the nasties you are trying to eliminate. It may well be worth investing in some new kitchenware, especially for those gf/cf items you intend to bake frequently, such as bread, biscuits and cakes. It is a sad reflection on my previous reluctance to cook that I had to buy some very basic kitchen equipment for the first time, rather than replace it.

- Utensils that are porous and will be used regularly, such as chopping boards, bread boards, wooden spoons, mixing bowls and plastic measuring jugs will need to be purchased and marked for gf/cf use only.

- Remember to wash and dry your hands thoroughly, as you move from preparing food for the family to gf/cf food. Gluten and in particular casein will be easily transferred from the sarnie you are preparing for yourself to the gf/cf sarnie you are making for your child.

- As cross-contamination can so easily occur during preparation and cooking, it is usually the wisest course to prepare/cook as much of the gf/cf food as possible first.

Cross-contamination will not, unfortunately, be confined to just your kitchen, where you are able to take steps to prevent such things occurring. There are other things that you will need to be aware of. Now some of these seem so obvious that you will question the necessity of them being here, but erring on the side of caution and being a firm believer that what is blindingly obvious to one person is not to the next, I'll include them. Some of them sound as if I've finally lost my marbles and have become totally paranoid, seeing crumbs of gluten and casein lurking everywhere, hell-bent on discovering the best way of being consumed by Jack. In the early days of the diet, I could have been found guilty of paranoia; my ignorance led on many occasions to me rejecting perfectly good food for Jack, because I thought it might contain something that might be related to gluten and/or casein. Maltodextrin is a good example of this. It has the word malt in it, malt contains gluten, and therefore I struck it off Jack's diet. Maltodextrin, I later found out, has absolutely nothing to do with either malt or gluten. In fact it is usually gf/cf, as it is derived from corn (UK maltodextrin only). So I am no longer paranoid, just overly cautious – something which I suspect you will become too. Once you have seen the good that this diet does and all the many wonderful changes that take place in your child, you will not want anything to happen that will undo all this good, least of all a silly mistake that could have so easily been prevented. So here is the list of the blindingly obvious or downright paranoid:

- Do not buy foods for the gf/cf diet that are from self-service, opened containers. You have no idea if a scoop from a gluten or casein-containing container will have accidentally been used in a gf/cf container.

- Do not buy bread, cakes, biscuits or any other baked goods from a bakery or supermarket that are labelled gf/cf, unless you are confident that they have been cooked away from the premises, in a bakery that only bakes gf/cf goods. I worked in a bakery in my student days, and it does not matter how scrupulous the bakery is about hygiene and cleanliness, there is no getting away from the amount of flour particles that are flying about the place. Even if the bakery insists that something is gf/cf, because it is the first thing baked each day, I would still have the greatest reservations about recommending it for any child on the diet.

- Eating out is a problem and it will probably always be a problem. Food that is deep fried will be contaminated by gluten and casein from the foods that have previously been fried in the oil. Even if the oil is changed, the fryer will still contain gluten and casein unless it has been scrupulously cleaned first. Grilled and fried foods are a problem for the same reasons. Even the good old British chip will often be coated in a gluten-containing powder, prior to the freezing process, for use in restaurants and cafés. Sauces, dressings and gravies are a no-no, unless you are prepared to go into the kitchen and check. Many, many foods that will be on the menu will be no good for the diet, as they will contain gluten and casein. Probably the best thing that you can do in this case is to inform the establishment at the time that you book the table that your child has many food allergies and ask if it would be all right for you to bring food for them with you. Then make a gf/cf meal that you know your child will eat, take it with you in a microwaveable container and ask the kitchen staff to reheat it for you and put it on a plate. At least this way, the whole family can go out for a meal together, even if it means that you will not get a rest from the cooking.

- As our lives seem to be increasingly revolving around fast food (and I don't know why this should be) and more and more children's birthday parties are held at either McDonald's or Burger King, this is an area you will need to be careful about. At the time of going to press, both McDonald's and Burger King are able to supply gf/cf burgers. But it is only at Burger King that you can be confident of ordering gf/cf fries all year round. At Burger King, they fry their fries in an allocated fryer; nothing else is allowed to be fried in this fryer. I got the distinct impression from talking to them that it would be a sacking offence to do otherwise. At McDonald's you can get the Hash Browns from their breakfast menu (they are egg free too!) and their fries. *But*, if they are running a promotion on other potato products (for example wedges or spiral fries), the fries and Hash Browns are off limits to a child on this diet due to the risk of cross-contamination. It is worth keeping on phoning their head office to check on any changes in practice. At both places you will need to be careful with the way you word your order, to ensure that you get a gf/cf burger. To get a gf/cf burger, you will have to adopt some Americanisms and ask for 'just a beef patty, no bun, with fries'. Ask for just a burger and that's exactly what you get, a burger, complete with bread bap. Also, all the tomato ketchup at Burger King (whether it is in sachets or single serving pots) is gf/cf. Your order may take a few seconds longer, as they will get you a freshly cooked burger (meat patty!) and not one that has already been stuck inside a bun and boxed up. Jack is very happy that he is still able to go to a Burger King or McDonald's and get a kid's meal complete with toy and it has made our life a little easier when we are going out for the day. Jack and Luke are both endowed with the instincts of a homing pigeon and are able to spot either Burger King or McDonald's long before an adult can.

- If your child attends playgroup/crèche/nursery, etc. and they have a break with drinks and biscuits, not only will you have to provide suitable alternatives for your child, but you will also need to explain that your child's biscuits will have to be kept in a separate container (it is best if you provide this) and that it will have to be served on a separate plate and handled before the other biscuits, so that it does not come into contact with gluten and casein crumbs.

The sneaky drug addict

One thing that you are likely to notice when you first remove gluten and casein from your child's diet is that they will do everything in their power to get hold of some. Remember the drug addict analogy: you've taken away their drug and they are going to do all they can to get some. They may not be stealing money from your purse to get their 'fix', but they are going to become very resourceful in trying to find some gluten/casein.

You will need to vacuum, and I mean really vacuum, all the rooms where food is prepared and consumed. That means getting all the attachments out and paying particular attention to skirting boards, under furniture (especially the sofa) and down the back and sides of chairs and sofas. Jack spent a good deal of his time during the first week of the diet combing the edges of the carpet and jamming his hands down the back of the sofa, searching for old biscuit/cake/bread/anything crumbs. No meal or snack at this time was complete unless I was there, waiting with a cloth to clear up immediately any spills of food that occurred and with a hand-held mini vacuum cleaner at the ready to vacuum around and under the dining table. Jack would often finish eating first and then hover around his brother, waiting to see where the crumbs would fall.

You will need to be very vigilant at meal and snack times, making sure that your child does not help themselves from the plates of others. Even if they have never shown the remotest interest in what the rest of the family are eating, you can bet that they will start to now. If your child moves faster than you and manages to grab some food, remove it immediately and wipe their hands, to make sure they will not get any gluten or casein by licking their fingers. If their knife, fork or spoon gets onto someone else's plate, remove it and replace it with another. Do this even if the food item they have managed to grab is gf/cf. Unless you are all eating gf/cf meals, there is every possibility that the gf/cf food has become contaminated by something else on the plate.

Do not be surprised if your child becomes totally enamoured with the kitchen and/or the kitchen cupboards. The kitchen, for those first few weeks on the diet, will be their idea of heaven, as everywhere they look there is food, and lots of it, that contains all those forbidden things that they are now craving. If you have not already childproofed your kitchen, it is a good idea to do this before you implement the diet. As you will not be able to watch your child 24 hours a day (do not dismiss the thought of midnight raids on the biscuit tin or bread bin), it is well worth your peace of mind to put child locks on all the kitchen cupboards and your fridge and freezer. Buy the most complicated and difficult-to-open child lock that you can get. As our children seem adept at opening the impossible, you may find that the lock isn't childproofed enough for your child, but it may buy you some time to discover what they are doing and stop them. One mother I know found that no lock was too difficult or too high for her son to open and eventually fitted all her cupboards with padlocks that could only be opened by a key (she was sure that he would soon be able to figure the numbers of a combination lock!) and kept the key out of sight and reach. I just made the kitchen a child free zone and fitted a bolt to the door that connected to the dining room and placed a child's safety gate at the other doorway to the kitchen. Jack did try on a number of occasions to 'break into' the kitchen, but soon got deterred and now doesn't bother. I now trust him enough not to take food, but I have found that I rather enjoy having a bolthole to escape to where the children can't get me and so I've kept the lock and gate where they are.

You may also find that your child may start to eat non-food items in their attempt to find some gluten and casein. Once they find out that they are not going to get their 'fix' from this non-food item, they will give up. So unless whatever they are trying to eat, suck or chew is dangerous, I wouldn't worry too much about it – they will stop soon enough. But you need to be on your guard, just in case they do manage to find some gluten or casein in a non-food item, play dough being an example of this. If your child likes using play dough, then before you begin the diet, throw away all the play dough that they have and thoroughly clean any tools they use with it and make up a batch of gf play dough (recipe in recipe section of the book).

The best time to start the diet

The best time to start the diet is, without a doubt, when you feel ready to. But there are times when starting the diet is not a good idea and other times when, depending upon your family circumstances, starting the diet will be better than others.

So first of all, the times when starting the diet is a bad idea, however enthusiastic/eager you are.

Starting the diet just before you go on a family holiday is not a good idea. Your child will need time to adjust to being gf/cf and while they are doing this, they are not going to be in a holiday mood. Unless you are going to go on a self-catering holiday, you will not be able to ensure that all your child is eating is gf/cf. Even if you are going on a self-catering holiday, the idea of packing a suitcase full of gf/cf food for your child is not very appealing, especially when you and your child are still getting to grips with what he can and cannot eat. Do not even attempt going on a holiday abroad when your child is still being weaned off gluten and casein. Unless you are completely fluent in the language of the country, trying to decipher the food labels and making catering staff aware of your child's intolerances is going to be a non-starter. And I can just picture the scene at the customs departments around the world as you try to explain that the holdall you are carrying, which is full of a suspicious looking white powder, really contains white rice flour that you need to make your child's bread. Well, if nothing else, it is probably a good way to get some publicity for the diet. I can see the tabloid headlines now…

It is also not a good time to start the diet a week or two before any major celebration, like Christmas, Easter or your child's birthday. Not only will your child not be in the best of moods, you will also find it unnecessarily stressful. You may well have locked your child out of the kitchen cupboards, but those chocolate novelties on the Christmas tree will disappear and you will find that the Easter eggs belonging to your other children will also 'vanish'. There is a company that makes gf/cf chocolate

Christmas novelties and Easter eggs, as well as gf/cf chocolate all year round. The details for D & D Chocolate can be found in the Specialist Suppliers Directory.

There are times, depending upon the circumstances of your family, which are better (for which, read less stressful) for starting to implement the diet.

Usually the best time to start the diet is during school holidays. Then you are able to monitor exactly what your child eats and drinks. Also at home, your child will be in an environment in which they feel the most secure, so that any symptoms that they might exhibit when withdrawing from gluten and casein will be easier for them to handle than if they are in an environment that they find strange or stressful. Personally, I also think it is asking a lot from any school, to try to implement the diet with you and cope with a child who is withdrawing from gluten and casein. At school there will also be more opportunities for your child to sneak some gluten and casein into their diet (play dough, playtimes, break times and journeying to and from school).

If your child is too young to go to school, then any time (apart from the ones listed above) will be a good time. The exception to this is if they have older brothers and sisters who are of school age. If this is the case, you may well find it easier to start the diet any time but the school holidays. By implementing the diet during term time, you can concentrate on your child and the diet. You will not be as distracted by the needs of your other children during the day as you would be if they were on holiday from school. It will also allow your child on the diet to go through any withdrawal symptoms with the minimum of impact on your other children.

Withdrawal from gluten and casein – what to expect

This, I'm afraid, is the million-dollar question. There seem to be no hard and fast rules about what you can expect when your child's body is getting rid of gluten and casein. Some parents report that their child seems to experience very little, others say that their child experiences a variety of symptoms, some of which are mild and others which are distressing to witness. There seems to be no rhyme or reason why this should be. It seems to be the wisest course to expect the very worst and then be pleasantly surprised. I really expected the first week to ten days (and nights) to be a living hell. It probably did not help that I had recently watched *Trainspotting!* In reality it wasn't the best time Jack and I had had together and I wouldn't want to go through it again, but it was nowhere near as bad as I thought it would be – perhaps we were just lucky. It probably also helped that I had adopted a 'siege mentality'. I cancelled all visits out, including playgroup and shopping (something that Jack has always found stressful) and no one was welcome to visit. I took the phone off the hook and steeled myself for *Thomas the Tank Engine* videos, from morning until night. In other words, I was planning to make the withdrawal period for Jack as stress free as possible, by keeping him in a secure environment.

If you are worried about what might happen during this period of withdrawal, do try to keep it at the forefront of your mind that an adverse reaction to the removal of gluten, casein, monosodium glutamate and aspartame from the diet means that your child is addicted/intolerant to these substances. Any such reactions are only serving to prove that you are doing the right thing by removing them from your child's diet.

If you are staggering the withdrawal of foods from your child's diet, i.e. taking out casein first, before the other substances, you will be unlikely to notice any withdrawal symptoms, as your child will still be getting their 'fix' from gluten. It will be when you fully implement the gf/cf diet that you will notice the withdrawal symptoms, but these will be less marked than if you remove gluten and casein at the same time.

Some of the withdrawal symptoms that have been reported by parents are (please remember that it is highly unlikely that your child will suffer from any more than a few of these):

- diarrhoea
- constipation
- stomach upset
- anxiety
- clinginess
- bad temper
- agitation
- disturbed sleep pattern

- lethargy
- hyperactivity
- running a temperature
- night sweats.

The Bad Guys

The following list is designed to help you, when buying food for your child, to spot those items which contain gluten and casein. I know that it is very long and daunting and is probably only serving to reinforce the ideas that the diet is too difficult and that your child will never be able to eat anything ever again. Please don't worry. Some of these ingredients you will never come across in your normal shopping, but it pays to be prepared. I have tried to make it as complete and comprehensive as possible, but I am sure you will appreciate that I cannot guarantee that food producers will not come up with ever more wonderful ways of describing gluten and casein.

To make life as easy as possible, I have made the list alphabetical and I have coded it for you, so that you know if the item refers to gluten (G), casein (C), or monosodium glutamate (MSG). I have marked certain items to let you know if a gf/cf alternative is available to buy (*). The items marked with a ? are usually derived from gluten or casein, but can be derived from a harmless source. These are best avoided until you have contacted the manufacturer to check the source of the ingredient.

THE KEY

G = contains gluten
C = contains casein
MSG = contains monosodium glutamate
* = gf/cf pre-made alternative available
? = can be from a source of gluten, casein or MSG, or may be fine.
Check with manufacturer before use.

Abyssinian (G)
Artificial cream (C/G)
Artificial sweeteners (C/G)

Baby foods (G/C *)
Bagels (G/C)
Baked beans (G *)
Baking powder (G *)
Barley (G)
Barley hordein (G)
Barley malt (G)
Barley sugar (G)
Barley water (G)
Barley wheat (G)
Batter (G/C)
Bavarian cream (C)
Burghul (G)
Binder (G)
Binding (G)
Biscuits (G/C *)
Blancmange (C)
Bleached all purpose flour (G)
Bouillon cubes/powder (G)
Bran (G) (except rice bran)
Bread (G/C *)
Bread rolls (G/C *)
Bread flour (G *)
Breadcrumbs (G/C *)
Breakfast cereals (G/C *)
Brioche (G)
Broth (G/C *)
Brown flour (G *)
Brown sugar (C ?)
Bulgar wheat (G)
Burgers (G *)

Butter (C)
Butterfat (C)
Buttermilk (C)
Butterscotch (C)
Butter oil (C)
Butter substitutes (C)

Cake decorations (?)
Cake flour (G *)
Cake mixes (G/C *)
Cakes (G/C *)
Calcium disodium (C)
Caramel colouring (?)
Casein (C)
Caseinate (C)
Cereal (G)
Cereal extract (G)
Cereal protein (G)
Chapattis (G/C)
Cheese (C *)
Cheese powder (C *)
Cheese slices (C *)
Cheese spread (C)
Chewing gum (G *)
Chicken nuggets (G/MSG but easily
   made)
Chips (G *)
Chocolate (C *)
Chocolate spread (C *)
Chorizo (G)
Ciabatta (G)
Clotted cream (C)
Coffee creamer (C/G)
Communion wafers (G *)
Condensed milk (C)

Cookie mixes (G/C *)
Cookies (G/C *)
Cooking chocolate (C *)
Cottage cheese (C)
Couscous (G)
Cracker meal (G)
Crackers (G *)
Cream (C *)
Cream cheese (C *)
Crispbreads (G *)
Crisps (C/MSG *)
Croissants (G/C)
Croutons (G)
Crumpets (G/C)
Curd cheese (C)
Curds (C)
Curry powder (G *)
Custard: ready-made/tinned/chilled/
    flavoured (C/G)
Custard powder (G/C *)

Delactosed whey (C)
Demineralised whey (C)
Dextrin (?)
Diglycerides (?)
Doughnuts (G/C)
Dried milk (C *)
Dry roasted peanuts (G/C)
Durum (G)
Durum wheat (G)

Edible starch (G)
Einkorn (G)
Enriched flour (G)
Evaporated milk (C)

Ewe's cheese (C)
Ewe's milk (C)
E621 (MSG)
E622 (MSG)

Faggots (G/C)
Filler (G)
Fish fingers (G/C/MSG)
Flavour enhancer (MSG)
Food essences (G *)
Food flavourings (G *)
Food starch (?)
Frankfurters (G/C *)
Fromage frais (C)
Fu (G)
Fudge (C)

Galactose (C)
Gelatine (MSG)
Gelatinised starch (G)
Germ (G)
Ghee (C)
Glutamic acid (G ?)
Gluten (G)
Gluten flour (G)
Goat's milk (C)
Graham flour (G)
Granary bread (G)
Granary flour (G)
Gravy (G/C/MSG)
Gum (?)

Haggis (G)
Herbs: dried/ground (G *)
High gluten flour (G)

High protein flour (G)

Hordein (G)

Hot chocolate (G/C *)

Hot dogs (G/C *)

HVP (MSG)

Hydrolysed plant protein (?)

Hydrolysed starch (?)

Hydrolysed vegetable protein (MSG)

Hydrolysed whey protein (C)

Hydrolysed whey sugar (C)

Ice cream (C *)

Ice cream cones (G)

Ice cream syrup (G *)

Ice cream wafers (G)

Ice lollies (G/C *)

Kamut (G)

Kibbled wheat (G)

Lactalbumin (C)

Lactalbumin phosphate (C)

Lactate (C)

Lactate acid (C)

Lactoglobulin (C)

Lactose (C)

Lactulose (C)

Lemon curd (C)

Liquorice (? * (see Glossary))

Lollies (G *)

Low fat milk (C)

Low fat spread (C)

Luncheon meat (G/C)

Malt (G)

Malt extract (G)

Malt flavouring (G) – see note

Malt syrup (G)

Malt vinegar (G)

Malted drinks (G/C)

Malted milk (G/C)

Margarine (C *)

Marzipan (G *)

Mayonnaise (C *)

Meatballs (G/C *)

Meatloaf (G/C)

Milk (C *)

Milk chocolate (C)

Milk powder (C *)

Milkshakes (G/C)

Milk solids (C)

Mincemeat – sweet (G *)

Modified food starch (?)

Modified starch (?)

Monoglycerides (?)

Monosodium glutamate (MSG)

Mousses (C)

MSG

Muesli (G *)

Muffins (G/C *)

Mustard powder (G *)

Naan bread (G/C *)

Non-dairy butter (G/C)

Non-dairy cream (G/C)

Non-fat milk (C)

Noodles (G *)

Nougat (G)

Oat flour (G)
Oat meal (G)
Oat milk (G)
Oats (G)

Pancakes (G/C *)
Pasta (G *)
Paste (G)
Pastry (G/C *)
Pâtés (G/C *)
Pearl barley (G)
Pepper: ready ground (G *)
Pies (G/C)
Pitta bread (G *)
Pizza (G/C *)
Plain chocolate (C *)
Plain flour (G *)
Popcorn: flavoured (C *)
Porridge (G/C *)
Potassium caseinate (C)
Powdered milk (C *)
Pretzels (G *)
Puddings (G/C *)

Quorn: flavoured (G/C *)

Rennet casein (C)
Rice malt (G)
Rice syrup (? worth checking as a lot
    of rice syrup is gf)
Rissoles (G *)
Rock (candy) (G)
Rusk (G)
Rye (G)

Rye flour (G)
Rye semolina (G)

Sandwich spreads (G/C *)
Sauce packet mixes (G/C/MSG *)
Sausage rolls (G/C)
Sausages (G *)
Scotch eggs (G)
Seitan (G)
Self-raising flour (G *)
Semi-skimmed milk (C)
Semolina (G)
Sheep's milk (C)
Shortening (C *)
Shoyu (G)
Skimmed milk (C)
Sodium caseinate (C)
Sodium lactylate (C)
Soups: fresh/canned/packet
    (G/C/MSG *)
Sour cream (C)
Sour cream solids (C)
Sour milk solids (C)
Soy protein extract (?)
Soy sauce (G/MSG)
Spam (G/C)
Spelt (G)
Spelta (G)
Spices: dried/ground/powdered (G *)
Starch (G ?)
Stock (G/C/MSG)
Stock cubes (G/C/MSG)
Strong flour (G)
Stuffing mixes (G *)
Suet (G)

Sweet whey (C)
Sweets (G/C *)

Taramasalata (G)
Teriyaki sauce (G)
Textured protein (?)
Thickener (?)
Thickening (?)
Toffee (C)
Tortillas (G/C *)
Tritical (G)
Triticale (G)
Triticum (G)

Udon (G)
UHT milk (C)

Vegetable protein (MSG)
Vegetable starch (?)
Vegetarian cheese (G/C *)
Vegetarian suet (G)
Vending machine drinks (G/C/MSG)
Vinegar (G ? *)
Vital gluten (G)
Vitamins (? *)

Wafers (G)
Waffles (G)
Wheat (G)
Wheat bran (G)
Wheat flour (G)
Wheat germ (G)
Wheat gluten (G)

Wheat malt (G)
Wheat starch (G) – see note
Wheat triticum (G)
Whey (C)
Whey protein (C)
Whey sodium caseinate (C)
Whey sugar (C)
Whey syrup (C)
Whipped cream (C)
White flour (G *)
Whole milk (C)
Wholemeal bread (G)
Wholemeal flour (G)

Yeast extract (MSG)
Yoghurt (C *)
Yorkshire pudding (G/C)

NOTES

Malt Flavouring is a substance derived from barley hordein. It is allowed by the Coeliac Society as being fine for coeliacs on a gluten free diet, but they note that a few coeliacs are unable to tolerate it. Many parents using the gf/cf diet have reported that their child has a problem with this. Malt flavouring is used primarily in breakfast cereals. Some of these cereals are promoted as being suitable for a gluten free diet, but this is a notice designed for the vast majority of coeliacs.

Wheat starch is the result of a process to remove gluten from wheat. It is now recognised that it is currently impossible for every trace of gluten to be removed from the wheat. In commercially produced wheat starch, there is a residual gluten content that is too high to be tolerated by both children on the gf/cf diet and coeliacs, therefore this must be avoided at all costs.

You will, however, notice that many foods labelled gluten free from specialist suppliers, contain wheat starch. This is a specially manufactured wheat starch that complies with the *International Gluten-free Standard* (*Codex Alimentarius*). This still contains a trace of gluten, but it is considered by the Coeliac Society to be safe for coeliacs to use.

Given that even wheat starch that complies with the Codex Alimentarius possesses traces of gluten, it may serve your child better if you choose foods that are made from naturally gluten free foods such as maize, rice, potato and soya. Again, the final decision is up to you.

The Good Guys

Having just seen such a long list of things that your child cannot eat on the diet, you are probably (and quite rightly) asking yourself, 'What on earth can I safely feed my child?' As a rule of thumb, the answer to this question is if it is not on the list of forbidden ingredients, then it is safe to assume your child can eat it.

There are lots of different foods that your child can eat. The list below is much smaller than the forbidden foods list, as it consists of actual foods rather than product descriptions which may well be disguising gluten, casein, monosodium glutamate or aspartame.

Gluten free flours

Buckwheat
Chickpea
Cornflour
Gram (chickpea flour)
Maize
Millet
Rice
Sago
Soya
Tapioca

The major food groups

Beans (beware of baked beans, some contain gluten)
Eggs

Fish (all fresh and unprocessed, some frozen – check, smoked fish can be a problem – beware of tinned tuna as it can be cooked in a solution that contains milk)

Fruit (fresh, tinned and some frozen – check. Be wary of dried fruits, which often have a gluten-containing substance added to stop them sticking together. Many children on the diet have an intolerance to one or more fruits. The fruits that are most likely to cause problems are: apples, bananas, melons, raspberries, grapes and all citrus fruits. The fruits that seem to be tolerated the best are pineapple, pear, strawberries (in moderation), apricots and peaches)

Meat (all fresh, some frozen – check. Cooked deli meat often contains milk derivatives. Processed meat can be bulked out with gluten and/or flavoured with casein)

Nuts (check salted, dry roasted etc.)

Poultry (most fresh (keep clear of basted and stuffed poultry), some frozen – check. Cooked chicken often contains milk derivatives. Processed chicken can be bulked out with gluten and/or flavoured with casein)

Pulses

Rice (some flavoured rice contains gluten or casein. Check frozen, cooked rice for added gluten)

Shellfish (all fresh, some frozen – check)

Vegetables (all fresh, most tinned and frozen – check)

Recipes

Gf/Cf Cooking

Without wishing to shoot myself in the foot, there is no real need to read this part of the book. With the exception of a few recipes, you can get just about everything you need elsewhere, without having to use my suggestions.

If your child eats meat, has no other allergies and doesn't suffer from candida, then you've got it made.

If your main meal of the day is a traditional English dinner – meat, potatoes, vegetables and gravy – all you need to do is make your child some gf/cf gravy and remember to mash the potatoes with gf/cf milk or margarine (the rest of the family will not notice, if you don't tell them). Finish the meal off with some gf/cf yoghurt or ice cream and it really couldn't be easier.

Even if your child is a vegetarian, has other food allergies or has candida, you can still get away with cooking very little in the way of 'special' food.

If your child is like Jack, and self-limits his food intake, then you probably don't have to cook much anyway or you cook the same thing morning, noon and night. So there is unlikely to be much change, apart from substituting gf/cf foods.

So why did I bother with this part of the book? There are several reasons:

- *Quality.* For example, there are many suppliers of good gf/cf bread (and just as many of poor ones, as far as Jack is concerned). I'm lucky enough to have found a good one that Jack likes and which I can get on prescription (my taste buds cringe when I remember the first gf/cf bread that I got for Jack to eat). But of all the breads I've tasted, be they ready-made, long life or packet mixes, none compare to the white bread recipe for bread machines that is listed below. It is true that unless you are a truly appalling cook, things do taste better when they are home cooked.

- *Choice.* Sometimes, there is only one possible gf/cf version of the food you need. Your child may not like it, or you might not have any in the kitchen cupboard when you need it.

- *Cost.* Some specialist gf/cf ready-made food is just too expensive to have on a regular basis. The case in point is biscuits. While I fully understand and appreciate why gf/cf biscuits are so expensive in comparison with normal biscuits (more expensive ingredients, fewer or no additives to extend their shelf-life, a production line set up solely for gf/cf foods, etc.), I cannot afford to feed Jack these on a regular basis. He takes gf/cf custard creams into his nursery, so that the biscuits he eats are like all the other children's biscuits, but at home he eats the biscuits that I make for him and his brother, which work out to be an awful lot cheaper.

- I wanted to prove to any of you who still doubt me just how easy it is to cook gf/cf foods. Some of the recipes, especially the main meals, shouldn't really be there. There is nothing special about them. They are either recipes I've been using for years (long before my children, let alone the diet) or they are recipes that have been very slightly adjusted, to substitute a gf/cf ingredient.

- *Quality control.* Some of the gf/cf foods (mainly those bought from a supermarket) may have ingredients in them which you are uncomfortable about giving to your child, or you may not be sure what they are, e.g. additives. At least if you are cooking the meal, you know what is going into it.

- You may just surprise yourself and enjoy cooking. Reluctantly, I can now hold up my hand to be counted amongst that number.

Now that I have, I hope, justified this part of the book's existence there are a few things that should be borne in mind before you get out your mixing bowl.

All of the following recipes have been tested and they have all had to meet some very tough criteria:

- They have to meet the requirements of the diet.

- They have to be as inexpensive as possible.

- They have to be as easy as possible to make. Trust me, if they have made it into this book, then they are easy, as I had to try to make them all first.

- They have to be as quick as possible to make. Life is just too short and mine is too busy, to spend more of it than I have to stuck in the kitchen, elbow deep in flour.

- Either myself or Jack or Luke were prepared to eat it. Jack, like many other autistic children, severely restricts the range of foods he will eat. Certain smells, textures, tastes and appearances put him off attempting to eat certain foods. It is getting slightly better and I live in hope that one day… Luke is almost a natural vegetarian. His own problems mean that he has great difficulty eating meat that is not either minced or highly processed. Which left me to eat most of the meat recipes.

- I am a great fan of anything that can be cooked in one saucepan or dish. I hate washing-up. A lot of the recipes will reflect this.

Before you start cooking

I apologise in advance for the fact that the flour and many of the other ingredients in the following recipes use American measuring cups as the measuring basis. It is pure laziness on my part. Measuring cups are very accurate. You fill them up and level them off with a knife. There is no squinting down upon a set of scales, to see if the little needle is lined up where you want it to be. Please use American measuring cups and not teacups; they aren't the same (I know it sounds obvious, but it wasn't to me!). The same goes for the teaspoon and tablespoon measurements.

Invest in some proper measuring cups and spoons. It really is worth it. You should be able to get both items from a kitchen equipment shop or a good department store. If you can't get hold of any, then contact Barbara's Kitchen (details in Specialist Suppliers Directory).

It really isn't worth trying to convert cups to ounces or grams, as cups are a measurement of volume and not weight. I have tried to do this and it is a disaster. For example, 1 cup of white rice flour weighs 4½ oz. So you would expect 1 cup of tapioca flour and 1 cup of potato starch flour to weigh the same, but they don't. 1 cup of potato starch flour weighs 4 oz and 1 cup of tapioca flour weighs 6 oz.

There are also recipes that are in the more traditional ounces. Again, it is all down to laziness on my part and the aforementioned difficulty in converting measurements from weight to volume and vice versa.

Nevertheless, no self-respecting recipe section is complete without a conversion table. So for what it is worth, here is mine.

Volume		*Weight*	
Metric	*Imperial*	*Metric*	*Imperial*
5 ml	1 tsp	25 g	1 oz
15 ml	1 tbsp	50 g	2 oz
20 ml	4 tsps	125g	4 oz
25 ml	1 fl oz	225 g	8 oz
50 ml	2 fl oz	350 g	12 oz
150 ml	¼ pint	400 g	14 oz
200 ml	7 fl oz	450 g	1 lb
300 ml	½ pint	700 g	1½ lb
450 ml	15 fl oz	900 g	2 lb
600 ml	1 pint	1 kg	2.2 lb
900 ml	1½ pints		
1 litre	1¾ pints		
1.1 litres	2 pints		
1.7 litres	3 pints		

Please note: If you are converting the measurements in a recipe, please be consistent and use either imperial or metric measures throughout the recipe, as they are not interchangeable.

All spoon and cup measurements are level, unless otherwise stated.

All cooking times given in the recipes assume that the oven has been preheated to the specific temperature. If using a fan-assisted oven, adjust temperature and time according to the manufacturer's instructions.

As all ovens vary, please check towards the end of the given cooking time to see if the dish is cooked.

Gf/Cf Baking

There are some simple rules that need to be followed when you are baking with gf flour.

When you bake with gf flour, the finished product is 'delicate'. The lack of gluten in the flours used means that the finished product is not as robust as you might have been used to with gluten-containing flours in the past. With cakes and biscuits especially, you need to wait for them to become absolutely cold (unless otherwise stated), before you try to remove them from the tray/tin. You will also need to line your tray/tin with greaseproof paper (unless otherwise stated), to help with the removal. If you don't, you will end up with a delicious tasting pile of crumbs. I have learnt this to my cost, several times. Luckily for me, Jack and Luke don't seem to worry too much about the presentation of their food. Just as well, because if they did, they would probably starve!

It is generally better, where possible, to make small baked goods rather than one large one, i.e. two 1 lb loaves of bread rather than a 2 lb loaf, or fairy cakes rather than a sponge cake. The texture is better and the product is not so fragile to handle. It is easier when you start making bread by hand to make rolls rather than a loaf. If the rolls do not rise too well, it is far less noticeable than if a loaf is looking flat.

Some of the recipes require you to roll out the mixture. This can be tricky. You will need substantial amounts of white rice flour, coating both the surface and the rolling pin, to prevent the mixture from sticking. When I am making small shapes, i.e. biscuits, I discard the rolling pin and break off small pieces of the dough and press it out using the flat of my hand. I find it is quicker and easier than rolling it out (and it saves on the washing-up!).

Please note: One of the flours used in the recipes is *potato starch flour,* this should not be confused with *potato flour,* which is far heavier than the starch. These flours are not interchangeable.

If your child is *allergic to corn,* you can substitute arrowroot for cornflour.

GF flour mix

In all of the recipes that call for a gf flour mix, this will always refer to the following flour mixture:

> 4 cups white rice flour
>
> 1 cup potato starch
>
> 1 cup tapioca starch

I make up a huge batch of this flour and store it in an airtight container, so that when I need to bake, I don't have to mix up the right quantity of the flour before I can get started. When the flour is mixed, I put it in the freezer. Seriously, I do store the flour in the freezer. Barbara, from Barbara's Kitchen, very kindly pointed out in the early days of my gf/cf baking that flour deteriorates very quickly. By freezing it, you prolong its life. The flour does not freeze together – it remains free flowing and I just measure out what I need and start baking with it. There is no need to thaw it.

Please note: If you are using a shop-bought ready-mixed gf flour for the recipes below, the results will vary, as it will contain different gf flours, in varying ratios, from the gf flour mix listed above. Some commercial mixes also contain various raising agents. The recipes below have raising agents as part of the ingredients, when they are needed. If you are using a commercial flour that contains raising agents, you will need to omit or reduce the raising agents listed in the recipe. As this can be tricky, and the end product may be significantly different from the desired result, I would recommend that until you feel you have mastered gf/cf baking, you stick with the gf flour mix formula given above.

Converting traditional bakery recipes

If you wish to convert normal bakery recipes to gf baking, then the following can be used as a guide only, when using the basic gf flour mix given above:

Plain flour mix

Makes 2 cups or approximately 8 oz

       2 cups gf flour mix

       2 tsps xanthan gum

Self-raising flour

Makes 2 cups or approximately 8 oz

       2 cups gf flour mix

       2 tsps xanthan gum

       1 tsp gf baking powder

For some recipe conversions, it may be necessary to add an extra ½ tsp of gf baking powder for every 2 cups of gf flour mix, to get the result you desire. It really is a case of experimenting. For some recipes, you may also need to increase the number of eggs that you are using.

Gf baking powder

Many brands of baking powder contain an additive (which contains gluten), to keep the baking powder free flowing. Some supermarket own brands are gluten free, but as they change all the time, it is not wise for me to list them here. You will need to keep checking with the supplier. There are many specialist suppliers who have gf baking powder, but if you are ever stuck you can make your own. It is very easy:

       1 part bicarbonate of soda and 2 parts cream of tartar

Breads

For companies who supply suitable ready-made or packet mixes of gf/cf breads, rolls, biscuits, pizza bases, etc., please refer to the Easy Reference Gf/Cf Foods Guide or the Specialist Suppliers Directory at the end of the book.

For the next three recipes I am grateful to Barbara Powell, of Barbara's Kitchen.

Barbara's white loaf, for bread machines

This recipe makes a 1½ lb loaf that is incredibly light and fluffy. The first time I gave Jack a slice of this, he was adamant that it was not bread, but cake. We have since come to a compromise and we now know it as 'bread cake'.

You are meant to leave the bread to get completely cold before slicing, but I defy anyone to wait that long. I can never resist the urge to cut off and eat a thick slice of this bread when it is still warm.

This recipe has the added benefit of making the very best breadcrumbs with which to coat chicken nuggets (see later recipe).

Dry ingredients

2½ cups white rice flour
½ cup potato starch flour
½ cup tapioca starch flour
1 tbsp xanthan gum
1 tsp salt
2 tbsps sugar
1 sachet (or 2¼ tsps) gf dried yeast

Wet ingredients

3 large eggs (at room temperature), beaten
¼ cup sunflower oil
1 tsp gf cider or gf white wine vinegar (optional)
½ cup soya or rice milk
¾ cup warm water

Method

- Mix all the wet ingredients together and place in the bottom of the bread machine.

- Gently mix all the dry ingredients (except the yeast) together and place on top of the wet ingredients.

- Sprinkle the yeast over the top of the mixture.

- Use the normal bake setting on your machine and choose the light or dark crust setting.
- When the bread is cooked, leave to cool for only a couple of minutes before removing the loaf from the tin, and place on a wire tray to cool.

Variations

- *To make a brown loaf, Barbara recommends adding 1 tbsp of molasses to the wet ingredients.*
- *Add 1 tsp of gf dried herbs or gf spices to make the savoury bread of your choice.*

Barbara's white bread or rolls – by hand

Dry ingredients
2 cups white rice flour
½ cup potato starch flour
½ cup tapioca starch flour
2½ tsps xanthan gum
⅔ cup dried gf/cf milk powder
1½ tsps salt
2–4 tbsps sugar

Wet ingredients
2 large eggs (at room temperature)
¼ cup sunflower oil
½ cup gf/cf milk
¾ cup warm water (hand hot)
1 tsp gf cider or gf white wine
      vinegar (optional)
1 sachet (or 2¼ tsps) gf dried yeast

Method

- Set aside 2 tsps of sugar.
- Mix all the dry ingredients together.
- In a separate bowl, dissolve the 2 tsps of sugar in the warm water. Then mix in the yeast.
- Slowly add the oil and vinegar.
- Using an electric mixer, slowly add the milk to the dry ingredients.
- When mixed thoroughly, add the eggs, one at a time. The mixture should feel warm.
- Pour in the yeast mix and mix in at the highest speed, for approximately 3–4 minutes.

- Cover the bowl and place in a warm place, until the dough has risen and doubled in size (this takes approximately I hour).

- Return the dough to the mixer and mix at the highest speed for 5 minutes. If you are doing this by hand it will require a strong wrist and take about 10 minutes.

- Divide the mixture between two 1lb loaf tins or put into a 2 lb loaf tin.

- Cover the tins and allow to rise in a warm place, until the mix has risen slightly above the tins (approximately 40–60 minutes).

- Bake the 2 lb loaf for I hour (the I lb loaf takes slightly less time), in a preheated oven (gas mark 6 – 200°C/400°F).

- To test if cooked, tap the base of the bread gently and listen for a 'hollow' sound.

- Remove from the tin immediately and cool on a wire rack.

Please note: Barbara points out that you may need to cover the loaves with silver foil after 10 minutes of baking to prevent the top of the loaf from overcooking.

For rolls

- *Place the dough into a strong plastic bag.*
- *Cut the corner off the bag and pipe out the desired shape of your roll onto a greased baking tray.*
- *Cover and allow it to rise (30–40 minutes approximately).*
- *Cook for about 25 minutes (depending upon the size of your rolls).*

Barbara's miracle gf/cf, sugar free and yeast free rolls

Barbara swears that this is a recipe for rolls. In this house we think that they are far too tasty to be rolls and for the last year, I have been passing them off to my boys as either English muffins or crumpets. Try them out, see what you think and then phone Barbara and tell her to come up with a less tasty roll recipe and rename this one 'crumpets'!

You can either use them as rolls, split them and toast them as English muffins, or if you want to have gf/cf crumpets, do the following. I have found that if you want to get a more 'crumpety' texture, with many air pockets in the finished product, it is best not to melt down the margarine. Instead break it down into small pieces with the back of a fork and add it at the end of the mixing process. As the crumpets (OK Barbara, the rolls) bake, the margarine will melt and leave air pockets behind. Absolutely perfect for trapping lots more jam in, after you've toasted them.

This recipe makes 4 large or 8–10 small rolls. They freeze well. I highly recommend that you make up at least double the mixture and freeze some (if your family leave you any to freeze, that is!).

Dry ingredients

I cup white rice flour
¼ cup potato starch flour
¼ cup tapioca starch flour
I ½ tsps gf baking powder
½ tsp salt
I tsp xanthan gum

Wet ingredients

I large egg, beaten
I tsp gf cider or gf white wine vinegar (optional)
3 oz gf/cf margarine (melted)
I cup water

Method

- Mix all the dry ingredients together.
- In a separate bowl, mix together the wet ingredients.
- Using a mixer on its lowest setting, combine the wet and dry ingredients.
- Divide between tins and bake for 18–20 minutes at gas mark 4 (180°C/350°F). If making smaller rolls, decrease the cooking time.

Variations

- *If your child has an egg allergy, Barbara says there is no need to use egg replacement powder, just add an extra ½ tsp gf baking powder and ½ tsp xanthan gum.*
- *Add dried fruit to the mix, for fruit muffins (Barbara suggests this, so in her heart of hearts, she knows this is too good to be a roll recipe!).*
- *This recipe also makes a good gf/cf pizza base. Barbara suggests adding a little less water and some gf dried herbs to the dough before baking.*

Microwave white bread

This bread works best if you use a container that has exactly a 1 litre capacity and is a loaf-tin shape. Other shaped containers mean that the bread will be too wide and shallow, so you will have to reduce the cooking time accordingly.

Ingredients

1½ cups gf flour mix
1½ tsps xanthan gum
1 sachet (or 2¼ tsps) gf dried yeast
1 tsp caster sugar

1 tsp salt
9 fl oz warm water
1 tbsp sunflower oil

Method

- Combine together the flour, xanthan gum, yeast, sugar and salt.
- Mix in water and oil to form a batter.
- Pour into a 1 litre (2 pint) microwaveable container.
- Allow mix to stand for 25 minutes in a warm place, to rise.
- Cook at full power for 8 minutes.
- Allow to stand for 5 minutes.
- Turn the bread out of the container and place in the oven at gas mark 7 (220°C/425°F) for 5 minutes to brown and crisp the outside.

Soda bread

Soda bread does not keep well and it needs to be eaten the day that it is made.

Ingredients

2 cups gf flour mix
1 tsp xanthan gum
1½ tsps bicarbonate of soda

1½ tsps cream of tartar
1 tbsp sunflower oil
2/3 cup cold soya or rice milk

Method

- Combine flour, xanthan gum, bicarbonate of soda and cream of tartar in a large bowl.

- Add the oil and rub it in with your fingers.
- Add the milk and mix in with a wooden spoon to create a stiff dough.
- Knead the dough into a ball.
- Place on a greased baking sheet.
- Cut a deep cross into the top of the loaf.
- Bake for 20 minutes at gas mark 7 (220°C/425°F).

Cornbread

This bread is popular in America. It is a very soft bread – so soft, that its alternative name is spoon bread. It is at its best served warm, on the day that it is baked.

Dry ingredients

1½ cups cornmeal/maizemeal
½ cup white rice flour
1 tbsp caster sugar
3 tsps gf baking powder
½ tsp salt

Wet ingredients

1 egg, beaten
1¼ cups soya or rice milk
1 tbsp sunflower oil

Method

- Combine all the dry ingredients in a large bowl.
- In a separate bowl beat the wet ingredients together.
- Gradually stir the wet ingredients into the flour mix, to form a smooth batter.
- Grease a 9-inch pie dish and pour in the dough.
- Bake in the top of the oven at gas mark 7 (220°C/425°F) for 30–35 minutes or until the top of the bread is beginning to brown.

Biscuits and Cakes

Rice crispy treats

If you hate the thought of having to cook, try this recipe. It is incredibly easy, takes next to no time and it will be an instant hit with your child.

It is based on a commercial recipe, without any of the forbidden ingredients, and costs a fraction of the price. Most marshmallows are gf/cf; I just use my local supermarket brand.

Ingredients

2 oz cf margarine
1 bag gf/cf marshmallows
Gf/cf puffed rice (e.g. Big Oz)

Method

- In a heavy-based saucepan (I use the pressure cooker pan) melt the margarine over a low heat.
- Reduce the heat to the lowest possible setting and add all the marshmallows.
- Keep stirring the mix until all the marshmallows have melted and are mixed in with the margarine.
- Remove from heat.
- Stir in puffed rice. Keep adding rice until the marshmallow mix cannot take any more (I usually then add another handful, just to be on the safe side).
- Line a baking tray with greaseproof paper. Spread the mix evenly over the tin and press down hard.
- As the mixture cools, it gets harder to spread; just dip a metal knife or spoon in some cold water and continue to press down.
- Cool in the fridge for approximately an hour, then cut into squares.
- Store in an airtight container, not the fridge, as this will make the squares go soggy.

Variation

- *Add 2 tbsps gf/cf cocoa powder to the marshmallow mix after the margarine and marshmallows have melted, and stir in well.*

Chocolate cornflake cake

This recipe is another really easy one to do and it doesn't involve any baking. It is also a good recipe to get the children to help with (if you are feeling brave enough!). A quick hint here: the better the quality of chocolate that you use, the more syrup you will need to add to compensate for the bitterness of the chocolate. Only add a small amount of extra syrup at a time and taste that you have the level right before adding the cornflakes.

Ingredients

I bar gf/cf chocolate
2 oz gf/cf margarine

2–3 tbsps golden syrup
Gf/cf cornflakes (e.g. Whole Earth)

Method

- In a glass bowl over a pan of hot water melt together the margarine, chocolate and syrup.
- Remove the bowl from the pan and stir in the cornflakes, making sure that all the cornflakes are coated in the mixture.
- Spread the mixture into a baking tray lined with greaseproof paper and allow to set in the fridge for 2–3 hours.

Variation

- *Works equally well replacing the cornflakes with gf/cf puffed rice.*

Jack's birthday biscuits

This biscuit is the result of me failing to convert a recipe properly. It was Jack's birthday and I was trying to do too many things at the same time. The resulting mistake was, much to my surprise, better than the biscuits I was trying to make. They got the thumbs-up from everyone who tried them, which includes those who were not on the diet.

They do have a very high sugar content, so I only make them on special occasions. The mixture makes so many biscuits that they seem to last from one special occasion to the next.

Ingredients

1 cup cf margarine
1½ cups caster sugar
1 egg, beaten

1 tsp gf vanilla extract
2½ cups gf flour mix
½ tsp xanthan gum

Method

- Cream together the margarine and sugar.
- Add the egg and vanilla and beat the mixture together.
- Add the flour and xanthan gum and mix together quickly with a wooden spoon, for no more than 2 minutes.
- Chill the mix for at least 3–4 hours in the fridge (better still, leave it overnight).
- Sprinkle your working surface with rice flour and roll out the dough until it is ½ cm thick. I found the mixture too fragile and sticky to roll out, so I cheated by pulling off small bits of dough and pressing flat with the palm of my hand, to the required thickness.
- Use cookie cutters to cut the dough. Again, I found the mix too fragile to make any shape apart from circles.
- Place on a cookie tray/baking sheet lined with greaseproof paper.
- Cook for 8–10 minutes at gas mark 4 (180°C/350°F).
- When cool, store in an airtight container.

Double chocolate chip cookies

These are truly wonderful American-style cookies and the perfect antidote to anyone who thinks that your child is going to be deprived on the diet. The recipe makes between 34 and 40 cookies, which is just as well, as they don't last long.

The chocolate that I use for all my baking is Supercook's Belgian Continental Chocolate. It has a cocoa content of over 70 per cent. The 75 g used for the recipe is half a bar. If the chocolate you use has a lower cocoa content than this, then you will have to increase the amount of chocolate you use accordingly. The chocolate is gf/cf, but the company will not guarantee this, as in another part of the premises they make a milk version of the cooking chocolate and this contains whey powder. There is a very remote chance of cross-contamination. So far I have had no trouble with the chocolate and I do use it a great deal. The chocolate is in a bar and so you will have to chop it into chips, but child that I am, I find this the best bit of the recipe! If this is far too strenuous for you, Plamil make carob 'choc' chips and D & D Chocolates make a gf/cf choc chip.

The cocoa powder I use is Cadbury's. It is 100 per cent cocoa and they guarantee it to be gf/cf.

Ingredients

1½ cups white rice flour
¼ cup potato starch
¼ cup gf/cf cocoa powder
2 tsps xanthan gum
½ tsp gf baking powder
1 tsp salt

1¼ cups caster sugar
1 cup cf margarine
2 large eggs, beaten
1 tsp gf vanilla extract
75g gf/cf chocolate chips (see above)

Method

- Combine the rice flour, potato starch, cocoa powder, xanthan gum, baking powder and salt in a small bowl.
- Cream the sugar and margarine together.
- Beat in the eggs and vanilla.
- Gradually add in the flour mix, and cream together.
- Stir in the chocolate chips.
- Roughly mould the mixture into small balls, between two teaspoons.
- Place the balls on an ungreased and unlined baking tray. The cookies will melt and spread out into traditional cookie shapes, during baking.
- Bake for 12–15 minutes at gas mark 5 (190°C/375°F).
- Remove immediately from the tray and cool on a wire rack.

These cookies keep well for several days in an airtight container.

Variations

- *Plain chocolate chip cookies: omit the cocoa powder and add an extra ¼ cup of rice flour.*
- *Plain vanilla cookies: omit the cocoa powder and chocolate chips; add an extra ¼ cup of rice flour and ½ tsp of vanilla extract.*

Viennese biscuits

This is yet another cooking mistake of mine. To be fair, I have admitted all along to being a stranger in my own kitchen.

I had started to make a cookie recipe I had converted, when I realised I had not got all the ingredients. So rather than throw away what I had already mixed, I improvised. The result was a biscuit that is very similar to Viennese whirl biscuits. So I made some cf 'butter' icing and sandwiched two biscuits together with some of the icing and a little strawberry jam.

I use cookie cutters to shape the biscuits, but if you want to be very professional, then put the mixture in a piping bag with a large nozzle attachment and make swirls on the baking tray. I have never tried this, as I don't own a piping bag and in this house these biscuits are eaten too quickly for there to be any appreciation of artistic design.

Ingredients

7 oz gf flour mix
½ tsp salt
½ tsp xanthan gum
½ tsp gf baking powder
3 oz caster sugar

3 oz cf margarine
I large egg, beaten
½ tsp gf almond extract
½ tsp gf vanilla extract (optional)

Method

- Mix together the flour mix, salt, xanthan gum and baking powder in a small bowl and set aside.
- In a large bowl, cream the sugar and margarine together.
- Mix in the egg and the almond and vanilla extracts.
- Blend in the flour mix.
- Cool in the fridge for 3–4 hours or overnight. If you are going to use the piping bag to shape the cookies, do this now, and then place the shapes in the fridge to cool.

- Roll out the mix until it is ½ cm thick (or use the palm of your hand, as for the double chocolate chip cookies, above). Use cookie cutters to shape.
- Place on a baking tray lined with greaseproof paper and bake for 8 minutes at gas mark 5 (190°C/375°F).
- When cool, sandwich two biscuits together with jam and 'butter' icing (see below).

'Butter' icing

Ingredients
1 oz softened cf margarine
Icing sugar

Method

- Mix in icing sugar, until you achieve the desired sweetness and consistency.

Note: If you need to keep sugar to a minimum for your child's diet, then it is possible to mix in cornflour with the icing sugar (no more than half and half), without the taste and texture being altered dramatically.

Vanilla and almond cookies

These are fairly plain biscuits which despite having a low sugar content are very tasty. This recipe makes approximately 25 biscuits.

Ingredients
2 cups gf flour mix
1½ tsps xanthan gum
½ tsp cream of tartar
½ tsp bicarbonate of soda

⅓ cup caster sugar
6 oz cf margarine, softened
½ tsp gf almond extract
½ tsp gf vanilla extract

Method

- Mix all the dry ingredients together well.
- Cream in the softened cf margarine, until all the ingredients are well combined.

- Add the almond and vanilla extracts and mix in well.
- Divide the mixture into 25 and shape into rough balls.
- Place the dough balls on a baking tray and squash each of them down slightly.
- Bake for 12–15 minutes at gas mark 5 (190°C/375°F).

Ginger cookies

These are really lovely cookies which only have a very mild ginger flavour (so if your child likes the ginger-ness of traditional ginger nuts, increase the amount of gf ground ginger by another ½ tsp). I now have to make a double batch of these cookies, as I eat so many that the children would not get a look-in. This recipe makes approximately 20 cookies.

Ingredients

4 oz cf margarine
1 tbsp golden syrup
6 oz gf flour mix
1 ½ tsps xanthan gum

1 tsp gf baking powder
½ tsp gf ground ginger
3 oz caster sugar

Method

- Melt together the margarine and golden syrup in a glass bowl, above a pan of hot water.
- Add all the rest of the ingredients and mix together well, using your hands if necessary, to form a firm dough.
- Chill the mixture in an airtight container for at least 1 hour in the fridge.
- Roll out the mixture and cut with a medium-size cookie cutter; place the cookies on a baking tray.
- Bake at gas mark 5 (190°C/375°F) for 10–12 minutes.

Variations

- *Omit the ground ginger and replace with ½ tsp gf ground cinnamon.*

Chocolate brownies

This recipe makes the chocolatiest brownies ever. It has been a big hit with all my chocoholic non-gf/cf friends.

I often make this in preference to a 'normal' birthday cake. I once made double the mixture and sandwiched the two huge slabs of brownies together with chocolate fudge sauce and fresh whipping cream, for a friend, as her birthday cake (she's not on the diet and so I broke the rules by adding the cream). She was amazed when I admitted to making it, as we had shared a house together for many years, and she was all too aware of my culinary limitations.

This is so rich that I cut the brownies into very small squares, about 1 ½ inches square, and this manages to keep everyone happy – even Luke, who would like to be a chocolate taster when he grows up.

Ingredients

⅔ cup cf margarine
150 g bar gf/cf good-quality plain cooking chocolate (see double chocolate chip cookies, above)
2 large eggs, beaten

1 cup caster sugar
1 cup gf flour mix
½ tsp gf baking powder
1 tsp xanthan gum
1 tsp gf vanilla extract

Method

- Melt the margarine and chocolate together, either in the microwave or in a glass bowl over a pan of hot water.
- In a separate bowl, mix together the eggs, sugar and vanilla.
- Add the chocolate mix.
- In a separate bowl mix together the flour, baking powder and xanthan gum.
- Stir the flour mix into the chocolate mix.
- Line a 9-inch square baking tin with greaseproof paper and pour in the mix.
- Bake for 40–45 minutes at gas mark 4 (180°C/350°F).
- Allow to cool completely before trying to remove from the tin. Cut into squares.

Scones

I have to admit that scone-making really is not my top bakery skill, so I was pleasantly surprised that these looked and tasted like scones.

Ingredients

2 cups gf flour mix
I tsp xanthan gum
2 tsps gf baking powder
¼ cup caster sugar

½ cup hard cf margarine
I large egg, beaten
3–4 tbsps soya or rice milk

Method

- Mix together the flour, xanthan gum, baking powder and sugar.
- Using your fingers, rub in the margarine, until the mix resembles fine breadcrumbs.
- Stir in the egg.
- Stir in the milk, until the mixture is soft but not sticky.
- Gently knead the mixture for about I minute.
- Roll out the mix until it is I ½ cm thick.
- Cut into circles with a large cookie cutter.
- Place on a baking sheet lined with greaseproof paper.
- Bake for 10–12 minutes at gas mark 6 (200°C/400°F), until well risen.

Shortbread

This recipe will not give you the very buttery taste of good-quality shortbread, but it is much, much better than almost all the commercial shortbreads on the market.

Ingredients

I ½ cups white rice flour
4 oz cf margarine, softened
2 oz caster sugar

Method

- Mix together the flour and sugar.

- Mix in the margarine by hand.
- Using the back of a wooden spoon, press the resulting breadcrumb-like mix into an 8-inch sandwich tin lined with greaseproof paper. Be brutal when pressing down the mixture or it will crumble when removed from the tray.
- Bake at gas mark 3 (170°C/325°F) for 40 minutes or until the top of the shortbread turns pale brown.
- Cut the shortbread while it is still hot, but do not attempt to take it out of the tray until it is completely cold.

American muffins

Dry ingredients
1½ cups gf flour mix
⅓ cup caster sugar
½ tsp xanthan gum
1½ tsps gf baking powder

Wet ingredients
2 large eggs, beaten
⅓ cup cf margarine, melted
⅓ – ½ cup fruit juice
1 tsp gf vanilla extract

Method

- Mix all the dry ingredients together.
- Mix all the wet ingredients together.
- Combine the two mixtures together.
- Spoon into muffin cases until they are half full and bake at gas mark 4 (180°C/350°F) for 15 minutes, until light brown.

Variations

The variations for this basic recipe are endless.

- *Add chopped, cooked fruit.*
- *Add gf cinnamon.*
- *If you are going to add gf/cf chocolate chips, replace the ⅓ cup of fruit juice with ⅓ cup of soya or rice milk.*
- *For double chocolate chip muffins, use 1¼ cups of gf flour and ¼ cup of gf/cf cocoa powder, then add choc chips. Replace the fruit juice with soya or rice milk.*

Basic Victoria sponge/fairy cake mix

Ingredients

1 ¼ cups gf flour mix
1 tsp gf baking powder
1 tsp xanthan gum
1 cup cf margarine

¾ cup caster sugar
2 large eggs, beaten
½ tsp gf vanilla extract
2 tbsps cold water

Method

- In a large bowl mix together the flour mix, baking powder and xanthan gum.
- In a separate bowl, cream together the margarine and sugar with a wooden spoon.
- Stir in the eggs, vanilla extract and water.
- Spoon the mixture evenly into two 7-inch sandwich tins lined with greaseproof paper.
- Bake at gas mark 5 (190°C/375°F) for 20 minutes.
- Wait until the cakes are completely cold before trying to remove them from the tins.

Variations

- This mixture also makes 24 fairy cakes. The baking time for fairy cakes needs to be reduced to 15 minutes.
- If you want to make a chocolate sponge, then replace ¼ cup of the gf flour mix with ¼ cup of gf/cf cocoa powder.

Breakfasts

Initially, the thought of providing a gf/cf breakfast can be daunting: 'Shall we have gf/cf toast or gf/cf toast?' But things aren't quite as grim as that. There is nothing wrong with a cooked breakfast, or eggs, boiled, poached, fried, scrambled, etc.

If your child has always enjoyed having cereal for breakfast, there is no reason for them to stop doing so, but of course, you will need to substitute a gf/cf version for their usual breakfast cereal. A word of warning here: many supermarket own brands of breakfast cereals are labelled gluten free, but they are not gluten free enough for your child. Most of these cereals contain malt flavouring. The cereal can be labelled gluten free, because malt flavouring is allowed by the Coeliac Society to be included in coeliac diets. But malt flavouring contains traces of barley hordein, and therefore it contains traces of gluten, so it is not suitable for our children. The same is true of major brand breakfast cereals that are labelled gluten free.

The good news is that there is a choice of gf/cf breakfast cereals. You can even get gf/cf porridge 'oats' made from flaked rice, and there is gf/cf muesli available too. For details of suitable breakfast cereals, please see the Specialist Suppliers Directory.

There are a variety of other breakfasts that you can make for your child and here are a few recipes to give you some ideas.

Pancakes and French toast

Pancakes make a great alternative to toast and cereal for breakfast, but in this house they are more usually eaten for tea. I've included two pancake recipes that are suitable for breakfast/tea time: the traditional English pancake, perfect for Shrove Tuesday (and every other Tuesday as far as I am concerned) and the smaller, thicker American-style pancakes, which are by far the favourites with my sons (and me too!).

I tend to make a double quantity of the American pancakes, as they freeze very well. You can either pop them into the microwave to defrost and warm through, or warm them under the grill on a low heat.

Although not breakfast pancakes, I've also included here two recipes for pancakes that are suitable for savoury fillings, as they are slightly thicker pancakes – buckwheat pancakes and spiced chickpea pancakes.

English pancakes

This mixture makes approximately 8 pancakes.

Ingredients
1 cup gf flour
¼ tsp xanthan gum
1 large egg, beaten
½ pint soya or rice milk

Method
- Mix the egg and milk together well.
- Add half of the milk mix to the flour and xanthan gum and mix together until smooth.
- Gradually add the remaining milk, stirring the mix well all the time.
- The batter mixture should be lump-free and runny; add more milk if necessary.
- For best results place the mixture in the fridge for 30 minutes before cooking.
- Cook as for normal pancakes.

American pancakes

Dry ingredients
2 cups gf flour
1¼ tsps xanthan gum
¼ tsp salt
1½ tsps gf baking powder
2 tbsps caster sugar

Wet ingredients
2 large eggs
1 cup soya or rice milk
2 tbsps sunflower oil
½ tsp gf vanilla extract

Method
- Combine all the dry ingredients in a large bowl.

- Combine all the wet ingredients in another bowl.
- Gradually add the wet mix to the flour mix, stirring all the time until lump-free. Use a wooden spoon for this, not an electric mixer or hand whisk. Be careful not to overmix the batter.
- This batter should not be runny. It should drop in one piece from a spoon, when the spoon is turned upside down.
- Add more milk if necessary to get the desired consistency.
- Heat a very little oil in a non-stick frying pan. Cook the pancake until small bubbles begin to form, and then flip it over.
- Do not be alarmed if these pancakes rise and look too high and thick during cooking. They will 'collapse' when taken out of the pan.

Filling ideas

- *Don't stick to traditional sugar and lemon for these pancakes. Try jam, maple syrup/honey, cooked fruit and ice cream. Yes, ice cream. Gf/cf ice cream and sorbet recipes are to be found later in this book. If you don't feel brave enough to make your own ice cream (but it is really simple to do), you can buy gf/cf ice cream (see Specialist Suppliers Directory) and several of the supermarket chains supply really nice gf/cf sorbets.*

Buckwheat pancakes

Ingredients
½ cup white rice flour
½ cup buckwheat flour
1 egg, beaten
½ pint soya or rice milk

Method
- As for English pancakes.

Spicy chickpea pancakes

Not a breakfast item, unless you like them to accompany the microwaved leftovers of the Indian take-away you are having for brunch! These make a thicker pancake than the traditional English pancake and they are great for wrapping up savoury fillings or using instead of pasta to layer between a meat and sauce mixture, like a lasagne.

These are also good to use as a chapatti or naan bread substitute.

Ingredients

I cup chickpea (gram) flour
1–2 tsps gf medium curry powder
I large egg, beaten

¼ pint soya or rice milk
¼ pint cold water

Method

- Mix the flour and curry powder together.
- In a separate bowl beat together the egg, water and milk.
- Add half the milk mixture to the flour. Stir together with a wooden spoon, until the mixture is smooth and lump-free.
- Gradually add the remaining milk mix, stirring all the time.
- Cook as for ordinary pancakes.

Sweet French toast

This was always a favourite breakfast of mine as a child and I did not lose the taste for it as I got older, I just stopped confining it to breakfast time! This was one of the very first things that I converted to being gf/cf. It is also a great way of using up bread that is no longer fresh enough for sandwiches.

Ingredients

2 large eggs, beaten
2 tbsps soya or rice milk
I tsp icing sugar
I large pinch of gf ground
    cinnamon (optional)

6 slices gf/cf bread
Oil for frying

Method

- Beat together the eggs, milk, sugar and cinnamon (if using).
- Soak both sides of each slice of bread in the egg mixture.
- Heat a very little oil in a non-stick frying pan. Use a low to medium heat setting; fry each side of the bread until it is golden brown.
- Serve immediately, either as it is, or with a little jam.

More substantial cooked breakfasts

Plain omelette

Ingredients

2 large eggs
1 tbsp soya or rice milk
Oil for frying

Method

- Whisk the eggs together with the milk.
- Heat a little oil in a non-stick frying pan, over a gentle heat.
- Pour the mixture into the pan, stirring gently to draw the mix from the sides to the centre, as the mix begins to set.
- When the mix has set, stop stirring and cook for approximately 1 minute more. It should be golden brown underneath and still creamy on top.
- Any fillings that are being added should be added now.
- Either turn the omelette over (you are on your own here, as I have never managed to do this without the omelette falling apart) or place the pan under a preheated grill to cook the top. If using the grill to finish off the omelette, take great care not to get the frying pan handle hot.

Suggested fillings

- *1 large pinch gf dried mixed herbs.*
- *2 oz thinly sliced, precooked mushrooms (not suitable if your child has candida).*
- *2 oz leftover cooked vegetables.*
- *3–4 oz gf/cf ham.*
- *2 oz gf/cf tuna and 1 oz sweetcorn.*

Potato and onion 'omelette'

This a very filling dish that serves 4–6 people. It can be served hot or cold. It is particularly nice cold, with a salad, for lunch.

Ingredients

1 ¼ cups gf olive oil
6 large potatoes, peeled and sliced

2 large onions, sliced
6 large eggs, beaten

Method

- Heat all the oil in a large non-stick frying pan.
- Stir in the potatoes and onions. Cover the pan and cook over a gentle heat, for approximately 20 minutes, until the potatoes are beginning to soften.
- Remove the potatoes and onions from the frying pan, with a slotted spoon to drain off as much oil as possible.
- Place them in a large bowl with the beaten eggs. Season the mixture and stir together gently.
- Pour off all but 4 tbsps of the oil from the pan and reheat the oil.
- When the oil is very hot, carefully pour in the mixture.
- Cook for 2–3 minutes, until the egg is nearly set.
- Cover the pan with a plate and very carefully invert the pan.
- Slide the omelette back into the pan and cook for a further 5 minutes.

Potato pancakes

This recipe makes approximately 8 pancakes. They are also good to accompany a main meal, rather than traditional mashed or boiled potatoes. They are suitable for freezing.

Ingredients

8 oz potatoes, peeled and chopped
1 large egg, beaten
2 tbsps soya or rice milk
4 tsps gf flour mix

¼ tsp salt
1 egg white
Sunflower oil for frying

Method

- Boil the potatoes until tender. Then drain and mash them.
- When the potatoes are cool, mix in the beaten egg, milk, flour and salt. Mix together well, until a thick, smooth batter is formed.
- Whisk the egg white until it forms soft white peaks, then carefully fold it into the potato mix.
- Heat some sunflower oil in a heavy-based frying pan.
- Add 2–3 large spoonfuls of the batter to the pan.
- Cook for 1–2 minutes each side or until the pancake is golden brown.
- Drain off excess oil on kitchen paper.

Lunches, Suppers and Snacks

You have trawled through the entire recipe section looking for just one recipe to make your life bearable on the diet. I should have it as the first recipe, but if I did, you would not have read the rest. Well, here it is…

Chicken nuggets

Please do not wait the eight months that I did to try this recipe. I thought it would be too difficult and fiddly and that Jack would reject it out of hand, like he does most other things. Well, I found out, when I finally got the courage to try it, that it takes 5–10 minutes to prepare and 8 minutes to cook. Oh yes, Jack loves them.

This recipe makes 12 good-sized nuggets.

Ingredients
1 uncooked breast of chicken, boned
   and skinned
1 large egg, beaten
Breadcrumb mix (see below)

Method
- Either cut the chicken into small, nugget-sized pieces or chop the meat up into tiny pieces and re-form them into nugget shapes.
- Roll each shape in the egg, and then roll it in the breadcrumbs.
- Reroll each shape in the egg and breadcrumbs. I find I have to push the breadcrumbs onto the chicken, by enclosing it in my hand.
- Cook under a preheated grill on medium heat for 4–5 minutes each side.

Fish fingers

Substitute for the chicken above ½ lb of white fish, filleted and skinned, and follow the method above.

Breadcrumb mixes

There are a huge variety of breadcrumb mixes. It is up to you to decide which one suits the recipe and your child the best.

The one that Jack loves

3 oz white gf breadcrumbs, I oz rice cracker crumbled and ¼ tsp gf garlic granules.

Or

4 oz white gf breadcrumbs and ¼ tsp gf garlic granules or gf celery salt.

Or

3 oz white gf breadcrumbs and 2 tsps sesame seeds.

Or

3 oz white gf breadcrumbs and I oz crushed gf cornflakes.

Or

2 oz white gf breadcrumbs, I oz crushed rice crackers and I oz crushed gf cornflakes.

Gf/cf batter mix

My thanks to AiA for this batter recipe. This is suitable for coating chicken or fish as an alternative to a breadcrumb coating.

Ingredients

9 oz gf flour mix
2 oz powdered gf/cf milk substitute
I oz granulated sugar
½ tsp salt

I tsp bicarbonate of soda
2 tsps gf baking powder
2 tsps egg replacer powder
   (optional)

Method

- Make up the milk powder and egg replacer as directed on the packet.
- Combine all ingredients together.
- Coat the meat/fish in the mixture and grill or fry.

Sausages

I do not for one moment suggest that you make your own sausages. Pure Organics make a gf/cf sausage which is available in most supermarkets and other varieties are available mail order (see Specialist Suppliers Directory).

You can also ask your local butcher to make them for you. First check that they make sausages on the premises (more and more butchers seem to buy them ready-made). Explain about your child's allergies and ask that your batch of sausages will be the first to be made at the beginning of the day (explaining about cross-contamination). Choose the meat of choice for your sausage, give your butcher a box of gf/cf puffed rice, and ask him to use the same amount of puffed rice as he would of rusk in the other sausages he makes. My thanks to Rosemary Kessick of AiA for this suggestion.

Burgers

Gf burgers are very easy to obtain. Nearly all of the supermarket chains do at least one own brand variety of gf burgers and Pure Organics (see Specialist Suppliers Directory) do a good organic gf/cf beefburger, which is available in most supermarkets.

I must admit, because my local supermarket makes a very good and reasonably priced gf/cf burger (which to Jack's delight is onion-less), I've only ever made burgers once, to ensure that this recipe worked.

This recipe makes 4 good-size burgers.

Ingredients

8 oz minced beef
2 thin slices of bread, crumbled into breadcrumbs, or ¼ cup cold cooked rice, or ¼ cup cold mashed potato

1 egg, beaten
1 small onion, finely chopped
Rice flour for coating
Sunflower oil for frying

Method

- Mix all the ingredients (except the rice flour and oil) together.
- Divide the mixture into 4.
- Using your hands, pat the mixture into burger shapes.
- Sprinkle each side lightly with rice flour.
- Fry in a little sunflower oil, for approximately 4 minutes each side.
- Drain off the excess oil on kitchen paper and serve.

Spicy tofu burgers

There are plenty of different tofu burgers on the market, but unfortunately all those that I've come across have gluten in them. These are a very tasty vegetarian burger. They are not suitable for freezing.

Ingredients

I large carrot or I small parsnip, finely grated

I large onion, finely chopped

I tbsp sunflower oil

I garlic glove, crushed

I tsp mild gf curry paste or gf ground cumin

8 oz gf/cf tofu

I oz gf breadcrumbs

I oz finely chopped nuts (optional)

White rice flour for coating

Method

- Heat the oil and fry the carrot or parsnip and onion for 3 minutes, stirring constantly.

- Add the garlic, tomato puree and curry paste or cumin. Mix in well and cook for 2 minutes.

- Mash down the tofu with a fork and then add it with the breadcrumbs to the vegetable mix.

- Mix all the ingredients together well, until they are combined.

- Divide the mixture into 8 portions and shape them into burger patties with well-floured hands.

- Fry the burgers for 4 minutes each side, until golden brown, or brush each burger with oil and grill for 3 minutes each side.

- Pat off the excess oil with kitchen paper and serve hot.

Pizza

There are loads of gf/cf pizza bases that you can buy (see Specialist Suppliers Directory for details). But making your own is cheaper and very quick to do.

For the pizza base, use either the dough from Barbara's miracle rolls (recipe above) or the following.

Ingredients

½ cup gf flour mix
½ tsp xanthan gum
½ tsp cream of tartar
½ tsp bicarbonate of soda

1 tbsp cf margarine
1½ tbsps cold water
Sunflower oil

Method

- Combine together the flour, xanthan gum, cream of tartar and bicarbonate of soda.
- Rub in the margarine, until the mix resembles fine breadcrumbs.
- Mix in the water, a little at a time, to form a smooth dough.
- Place dough on a baking tray lined with greaseproof paper, and with the palm of your hand, press out the dough until it is a flat circle.
- Brush the top of the pizza dough with a little sunflower oil.
- Add the topping of your choice and bake at the top of the oven for 15–20 minutes at gas mark 7 (220°C/425°F).

Suggested toppings

- Any of the pasta sauces (recipes under Main Family Meals).
- Vegetable medley (recipe below).

Vegetable medley

This also makes a good vegetable side dish, or goes with rice as a main meal. If you are using this as a pizza topping, make it while the pizza base is cooking and spread it over the top when both are ready. There is no need to grill or bake further, unless you are adding gf/cf ham and/or gf/cf cheese. For suitable cheeses, please refer to Specialist Suppliers Directory. If your child has candida, omit the mushrooms.

Ingredients

14 oz tin chopped tomatoes
¼ tsp gf dried mixed herbs
1 onion, grated
1 garlic clove, crushed
2 celery sticks, thinly sliced
1 pepper, diced

1 tsp caster sugar
2 tsps gf/cf tomato ketchup
12 oz tin sweetcorn
4 oz button mushrooms, thinly sliced

Method

- Lightly fry the onion, garlic, pepper, celery, herbs and mushrooms for 3–4 minutes.
- Add the tomatoes, sugar, ketchup and sweetcorn. Mix in well and simmer for 5 minutes.

Speedy sausage 'rolls'

Scandic do a good frozen frankfurter that is gf/cf, yeast and soya free and also free from genetically modified ingredients. Pure Organics do a pork sausage that is gf/cf. Both of these are available in most supermarkets. See Specialist Suppliers Directory for other suppliers of gf/cf sausages.

Ingredients

Sliced gf/cf bread
Precooked gf/cf sausages/frankfurters

Cf margarine
Gf/cf tomato ketchup (optional)

Method

- Cut off the crusts from the bread, then flatten out the bread, using a rolling pin.
- Cut the sausages into the required length.
- Cut the bread into long strips, slightly narrower than the cut sausage.
- Spread the bread lightly with tomato ketchup, if wished.
- Wrap the bread around the sausage and secure with a cocktail stick.
- Melt the margarine and brush it over the outside of the bread.
- Bake for 10 minutes at gas mark 5 (190°C/375°F).

Speedy chicken 'pie'

This is a non-cook recipe. The mixture below will fill two individual pie tins. If you cannot get hold of a gf/cf mayonnaise (Hellmann's Original Mayonnaise is gf/cf), then you can make your own (see recipe below).

Ingredients

1 celery stick or 2 spring onions, finely chopped

2 tbsps sweetcorn

2 tbsps gf/cf mayonnaise

4 oz cold, cooked chicken, finely chopped

1 packet gf/cf plain crisps, crushed

Method

- Mix all the ingredients, except the crisps, together.
- Spoon the mixture evenly between two small pie tins.
- Sprinkle the crisps over the top, when ready to serve.

Variations

- *Substitute ham or bacon for the chicken.*
- *Top the 'pie' with mashed potato (mash the potatoes with a little cf margarine).*

Soups

It is very hard to track down in supermarkets a soup that is gf/cf and free from MSG. The Directory at the back of the book lists the specialist retailers which stock soups that are suitable for the diet.

Home-made soups are far superior in every way to tinned and packet soups, especially if they are made with a home-made stock. Most soups freeze well (the two listed below do), but use a shallow container to freeze, as this will greatly speed up the defrosting process. Defrost overnight at room temperature.

Soups are a great way of getting children to eat a variety of meats and vegetables. If your child does not like different textures in a meal, then blend the soup down until it is a smoother consistency. Jack still will not eat it like this, but it did the trick when Luke was going through a strange spell with food as a toddler.

There are lots of soup recipes that are easy to convert to gf/cf. But I wouldn't try any of the creamed soups. You can make them with soya or rice milk, but they are anything but creamy. You can use Provamel's cream alternative (soya based), as a substitute for normal cream, but add it just before serving to prevent it separating. I've simply put in two soup recipes that are really filling and were enjoyed by us, even before we began the diet.

If you like croutons in your soup, cut slightly stale gf bread into cubes and fry in oil until crisp and golden brown. To make them even tastier add a few gf garlic granules to the oil.

Minestrone

This is a real meal in itself and far too good just to be restricted to a meal for the diet. This makes 4 generous adult-size portions and is even better when it is heated up again the next day.

Ingredients

1 large onion, chopped
2 carrots, thinly sliced
1 leek, sliced
1 large potato, thinly sliced
4 oz gf/cf bacon, diced
2 oz cf margarine
1 garlic clove, crushed
2 oz frozen peas

1½ pints beef or vegetable stock (see recipes below)
1 tbsp gf/cf tomato puree
1 tsp dried gf basil or oregano
3 oz gf spaghetti pasta
1 oz white rice
14 oz tin of tomatoes

Method

- Fry the bacon, garlic and onion in the margarine for 5 minutes.
- Stir in the carrots, leeks and peas. Cook for 5 minutes.
- Stir in stock, potatoes, tomato puree and herbs. Season and bring to the boil.
- Cover the pan and simmer for 5 minutes.
- Add the pasta, rice and tinned tomatoes and simmer for a further 15 minutes.
- Remove from heat and serve.

Mixed bean and vegetable soup

This is another hearty soup, vegetarian this time. It blends down really well to a thick smooth paste, and so is good if your child has a problem with different textures.

Ingredients

1 onion, chopped
½ lb potatoes, diced
1 carrot, finely sliced
1 parsnip, finely sliced
1 pepper, diced
2 celery sticks, chopped
1 tbsp sunflower oil
1 garlic clove, crushed
2 pints gf/cf vegetable stock (see recipe below)

15 oz tin of kidney beans, drained and rinsed
15 oz tin of black-eyed beans, drained and rinsed
1 courgette, sliced
1 tsp gf mild curry powder (optional)

Method

- Heat oil in a large, heavy-based saucepan (a pressure cooker pan is perfect).
- Add all the vegetables except the courgette and the beans. Cook on a high heat for 5 minutes, stirring constantly.
- Add curry powder and garlic and continue to cook for a further 3 minutes.
- Add the stock. It should cover the vegetables; if it doesn't, then add more.
- Bring to the boil. Reduce heat, cover and simmer for 20 minutes.
- Add beans, then continue to cook for a further 10 minutes.
- Remove half of the soup and puree it in a blender.
- Return the puree to the soup and bring the mixture back up to the boil.
- Add the courgette and seasoning and then simmer for 4–5 minutes, until the courgette is tender.
- Add a little water or extra stock if necessary to thin down the soup.

'Instant' vegetable soup

This is nowhere near as tasty as the previous two soup recipes, nor would it rate highly as a nutritious meal. But for those days when time has run out, it is a good enough alternative.

Ingredients
½ pint gf/cf stock of choice
3 oz mixed vegetables (frozen or tinned)

Method
- Place all ingredients in a microwaveable jug.
- Cook on full power for 2 minutes if the vegetables are frozen or 1 minute if the vegetables are tinned.
- Stand for 2 minutes before serving.

Stocks

Why bother with home-made stocks? I know, they are time consuming and fiddly, life is too short, etc. The strange thing is, they are not time consuming at all, unless you consider chopping up a few vegetables, throwing them in a saucepan full of water and leaving them to simmer for an hour or two, fiddly and time consuming. As to the 'why bother?', if you taste the difference between the home-made and the powdered/cubed commercial varieties, you will have your answer. They really don't stand the comparison.

Most importantly for the gf/cf diet, at the time of going to press I could not find a stock that was suitable for the diet. Although gluten and casein free stocks do exist, unfortunately I could not find one that was also free of yeast extract or HVP. As both these substances contain naturally occuring MSG they are not suitable for inclusion.

The three stock recipes below can be kept in the fridge for up to three days. All of them freeze well. I tend to freeze them in ice cube trays first and then put them in a suitable container. It just means they thaw quicker and I can use as much or as little as I need for a recipe. I also 'cheat' a lot now and my stocks are generally made up of the leftovers of a roast dinner. It cuts down the preparation time still further.

Chicken stock

Makes approximately 1½ pints

Ingredients

Whole chicken carcass (with some meat still attached)
1 large onion, sliced
2 carrots, sliced
2 celery sticks, chopped
1 bay leaf or gf bouquet garni
3 pints water

Method

- Break up the carcass into a large saucepan and add the water, vegetables and herbs. Stir well.

- Bring the stock to the boil, and then reduce the heat. Partially cover and simmer for 2 hours.

- Remove from heat and skim off the fat/scum that has risen to the surface.

- Strain the stock through a fine sieve and allow the liquid to cool.

- When it is cold, scoop off the fat.

Beef stock

Makes approximately 1½ pints.

This is meant to be made with 1 lb of shin of beef on the bone. Since the advent of BSE, it has become impossible to get beef on the bone. Either the leftovers of roast beef or stewing steak does the job nicely. In fact the cheaper, fattier cuts of beef are the best to use for a tasty beef stock.

Ingredients

1 lb beef, roughly diced
1 onion or 2 leeks, chopped
1 carrot, chopped
2 celery sticks, chopped
1 gf bouquet garni
3 pints water
Sunflower oil

Method

- Heat a little sunflower oil in a large saucepan and brown the meat.
- Add the water, vegetables and herbs and stir well.
- Bring to the boil, reduce heat and partially cover the pan.
- Simmer for 2 hours.
- Remove from heat and skim off the fat and scum.
- Strain through a fine sieve and allow the liquid to cool.
- When cold, scoop off the fat.

Vegetable stock

Makes approximately 2½ pints.

Ingredients

1 large onion
2 carrots
1 leek
3 celery sticks

1 turnip
1 parsnip
1 gf bouquet garni
3 pints water

Method

- Chop up all the vegetables.
- In a large saucepan, add all the ingredients and stir.
- Bring to the boil. Partially cover and simmer for 1 hour.
- Remove from heat and remove all the scum from the top.

Main Family Meals

Once you get the hang of the diet, main meals that all the family can eat together are easy to convert/prepare. It is a good idea to make one meal that all the family can eat. Not only will it save you time and money, but it will also make your child feel less different. Even though Jack severely restricts his range of foods, I do try as often as possible to ensure that the rest of the family eats the same or similar.

As I have said before, you will not be harming any other members of your family by giving them gf/cf foods. In fact, when you consider the amount of fat you can cut out of the family diet by limiting dairy products for everyone, you will only be doing them good. The same goes for reducing the gluten content in the diet. When you think how much gluten-based goods are used to bulk out commercially prepared food, you won't be doing anybody any harm by reducing them.

To get you started on family-based gf/cf meals, here are a few ideas.

Rice-based dishes

All of these dishes have rice as their main component. There is no need to get any gf/cf substitute. Rice is gf/cf, as long as it has not been flavoured with anything. Whether you choose white or brown rice is up to you.

Surprisingly, many supermarket and well-known brands of Chinese cooking sauces are gf/cf and MSG free. The same is true for Indian and curry sauces. If your child is willing to eat stir-fries and/or curries, then life on this diet will be very easy for you.

If, like me, your rice ends up looking nothing like the fluffy, individually separated, plump grains on the rice packet, you may want to invest in a rice cooker. They are readily available in most catalogues and department stores, and they have come down in price a lot over the last couple of years. They are simple to use and really take the guesswork out of rice cooking. Alternatively, there are lots of ready-cooked frozen rices on the market, but you will need to check these to make sure that they do not include a gluten-containing substance that allows the rice to remain separate and flow freely even when frozen.

Speedy tuna risotto

This is yet another recipe that doesn't deserve to be called one — it is so easy and quick to do. This makes 2 child-size portions.

Ingredients

½ onion, finely chopped
4 oz rice
4 oz tin mixed vegetables
I clove garlic, crushed

7 oz tin tuna
I pint water
4 tsps gf/cf tomato ketchup
   (optional)

Method

- Fry the onion, until soft.
- Add the rice, vegetables, garlic, ketchup and water.
- Bring to the boil and simmer for 10 minutes.
- Add tuna, stir in well. Heat the tuna through and serve.

Variation

- *Replace the tuna with gf/cf ham or precooked turkey or chicken.*

Spinach and bacon risotto

Ingredients

I large onion, finely chopped
I clove garlic, crushed
8 oz rice
I ½ pints gf/cf vegetable or chicken stock
   (see previous section for recipe)

8 oz bacon
4 oz spinach, washed and
   shredded

Method

- Chop and fry the bacon until it is crispy.
- Add the spinach and stir until the spinach is wilted. Drain off excess oil and put to one side.

- Gently fry the onion until soft, then add the garlic.
- Stir in the rice and gradually add the stock. Bring to the boil, then immediately reduce heat to the lowest setting.
- Allow the rice to simmer gently until almost all the liquid has been absorbed. Do not cover the pan and do not stir the rice.
- Add the bacon and spinach. Mix in well and serve immediately.

Greek risotto

Ingredients

4 tbsps sunflower oil
1 onion, chopped
1 red pepper, chopped
1 green pepper, chopped
12 oz rice

8 oz tin chopped tomatoes, drained
1½ pints gf/cf vegetable stock (see above for recipe)
5 oz frozen peas

Method

- Gently fry the onion in the oil until soft.
- Add peppers and cook for a further 3 minutes.
- Add the rice and stir in well, until the rice is coated in the oil.
- Add tomatoes and stock.
- Keeping the pan at a low heat, cook until the stock has been absorbed (approximately 20 minutes).
- Add peas and any seasoning. Stir in and wait 2–3 minutes, until the peas are cooked.
- Serve immediately.

Tuna and vegetable rissoles

Makes 12

Ingredients

4 oz rice, cooked
7 oz tinned tuna, drained
1 carrot
1 courgette
1 potato
1 onion

2 oz gf/cf breadcrumbs
1 egg, beaten
7 oz tin creamed sweetcorn
½ tsp gf dried parsley
3 tbsps white rice flour

Method

- Place the carrot, courgette, potato and onion into a blender and roughly blend together.
- Mix the tuna, sweetcorn, breadcrumbs, parsley and blended vegetables into the rice.
- Bind the mixture together with the egg.
- Divide the mixture into 12 and using your hands, roll it into burger shapes.
- Dip each rissole in flour, coating both sides.
- Fry for 3 minutes each side.

Special fried rice

Ingredients

8 oz rice
3 oz bean sprouts
1 large carrot, coarsely grated
4 spring onions, chopped into large pieces

2 oz prawns
1–2 tbsps sunflower oil
1–2 cloves garlic, crushed
3 oz frozen peas

Method

- Cook the rice until almost tender, then drain and rinse through with boiling water.
- Leave to cool. Spreading it out on a plate will speed this up.
- In a wok or large frying pan, heat the oil and cook the carrots and garlic for 2 minutes.
- Add the prawns, peas and bean sprouts and cook for a further minute.
- Add the rice and spring onions, cook for 3 minutes.
- Serve immediately.

Variations

- *The variations for this are almost endless. Any chopped, cooked meats and vegetables can be added.*

Egg fried rice

Ingredients

12 oz rice, cooked and cooled
2 eggs, beaten
1 tsp sugar

1 tsp gf garlic granules (optional)
1–2 tbsps sunflower oil

Method

- Heat the oil in a wok or large frying pan.
- Pour the egg into the wok, in a slow and thin stream, stirring it constantly, so that the egg breaks into small pieces as it cooks.
- Add the sugar (and garlic) and rice and mix in well.
- Continue to cook until the rice is heated through.
- Add a little extra oil if the rice begins to stick.
- Serve immediately.

Pasta dishes

Pasta dishes are easy to do. To make the meal gf/cf, all you have to do is cook some gf pasta for your child and add one of the following sauces. There is a huge range and variety of gf pasta. They basically fall into three groups, those made from soya, those made from corn/maize and those made from white or brown rice. There are as many different shapes and colours as normal pasta, so there should be no difficulty in choosing one that matches the pasta the rest of the family are eating. Which you choose is up to you and your child's preference. If you are confused about which to try initially, I would recommend trying pasta made from white rice. It has no flavour of its own and even Jack will eat a little of it. I've yet to manage to get him to eat a pasta sauce. He prefers to mix in a bit of tomato ketchup and have his favourite meatballs, set to one side of the plate.

Hardly as tasty and nutritious as the spaghetti bolognese we're tucking into, but at least he is moving in the right direction.

When buying gf pasta, it does pay to shop around. Although the quality of the pasta varies very little from suppliers, the price does. When comparing prices, remember to compare the weights as well, as these too vary enormously from supplier to supplier.

If your child likes white rice pasta, you could be onto a real financial winner. Sharwood's make a white rice noodle that is gf/cf, and it's available in every supermarket I've ever been in.

When it comes to ready-made gf/cf, while MSG free pasta sauces are available, there is not as much choice of varieties as there are with Chinese and Indian sauces. But one that is and is also easy to get hold of in supermarkets, is Dolmio Original Sauce for Bolognese (please check ingredients when you purchase, in case they have changed the recipe since this book was published). Being the lazy cook that I am, I rely on this sauce a lot and just jazz it up with a variety of different meats and vegetables thrown in.

Some of your children may have a problem with tomatoes. I don't know if Jack has this problem too, as so far I have never been able to get him to eat anything that contains tomatoes (is he trying to tell me something?), with the exception of tomato ketchup. As pasta sauces traditionally rely heavily upon tomatoes and tomato puree, you may be inclined to think that pasta dishes are not suitable for your child; please don't. You can make perfectly acceptable pasta sauces following the recipes below, omitting the offending tomatoes and tomato puree and substituting gf/cf white sauce (recipe to follow).

You can throw all sorts of ingredients into the two basic tomato sauces: bacon, mince, vegetables, ham, chicken, etc. Both sauces freeze well, so it's worth making a double batch that you can add leftovers to. The first sauce is the easiest, in terms of ingredients used, and there is no blender to wash up. The second is a more authentic, rich, tomato sauce. Both are delicious, but no prizes for guessing which one I use!

Basic tomato sauce for pasta 1

Ingredients

1 onion, finely chopped
2 cloves garlic, finely chopped
2 14 oz tins tomatoes

2 tbsps tomato puree
1 tsp caster sugar
½ tsp gf dried mixed herbs/oregano

Method

- Gently fry the onion and garlic for 5 minutes.
- Add the tomatoes, tomato puree, sugar and herbs.
- Simmer on a low heat for 20 minutes.

Basic tomato sauce for pasta 2

Ingredients

½ onion, finely chopped
2 celery sticks, finely chopped
2 oz sun-dried tomatoes, finely chopped
2 cloves garlic, crushed

2 14 oz tins chopped tomatoes
2 tbsps gf tomato puree
¼ pint gf/cf vegetable stock (see
    recipe above)

Method

- Very gently fry the onions, celery and garlic for 5 minutes, until soft.
- Add the tins of tomatoes, cover pan and simmer for 3 minutes.
- Add the sun-dried tomatoes, tomato puree and stock, stir well and cook for 5 minutes.
- Puree mix in a blender, and season to taste.

Spaghetti bolognese

Ingredients

1 lb minced beef
Tomato sauce (see above)

Method

- Fry the mince on a gentle heat, until browned. Drain off excess oil.
- Add sauce to the mince, cook for a further 20 minutes.

Variations

- Substitute minced chicken, turkey, bacon or sliced cooked gf/cf sausages for the minced beef.

White sauce

Makes ½ pint

Ingredients
2 tbsps cornflour
½ pint soya or rice milk
I tbsp cf margarine

Method

- In a cup or small bowl, mix the cornflour with 4 tbsps of the milk into a smooth paste.
- Place the remaining milk in a saucepan and bring to the boil.
- Add the cornflour paste, stirring or whisking vigorously to prevent lumps.
- Bring the sauce back up to boiling, stirring continuously, until it thickens.
- Reduce heat, and cook for a further 2–3 minutes.
- Stir in the margarine. When it has melted, serve.

Variation

- A quick pasta sauce using this white sauce can be made by adding some sautéed finely chopped onions and thinly sliced mushrooms. A sprinkle of gf garlic granules adds extra flavour too.

White bean pasta sauce

Ingredients

I large onion, sliced
2 cloves garlic, crushed
½ tsp gf dried mixed herbs

14 oz tin cooked cannelloni beans
14 oz tin chopped tomatoes
12 oz gf/cf pasta, cooked

Method

- Gently fry the onions and garlic for 10 minutes.
- Add the beans, tomatoes and herbs, cook for 5 minutes.
- Stir in the pasta and serve.

Aubergine bolognese sauce

Ingredients

2 aubergines, cubed
I red pepper, chopped
I yellow pepper, chopped
2 leeks, sliced
2 carrots, thinly sliced
2 cloves garlic, crushed

5 oz tin sweetcorn
4 oz red lentils
2 14 oz tins tomatoes
I pint gf vegetable stock
½ tsp gf dried mixed herbs

Method

- Gently fry the aubergines, peppers, leeks and carrots for 3 minutes.
- Add the garlic, sweetcorn, lentils, tomatoes, stock and herbs. Stir in well.
- Bring the sauce mix to the boil. Reduce heat, cover the pan and simmer for 30 minutes.

Meatballs and falafels

Italian meatballs

These are delicious when served with either of the two tomato sauces. When the sauces are ready, add the meatballs and cook in the sauce for a further 20 minutes.

Jack will eat these. But if you don't fancy making your own meatballs, you can buy from supermarkets good gf/cf meatballs made by a company called Scan, called Authentic Swedish Meatballs. They are made from pork and beef and they don't contain any yeast extract. You will find them in the chilled food cabinet. Jack lived on these and very little else for months.

Ingredients

I lb mince
I small onion, finely chopped

½ tsp gf dried mixed herbs
¼ tsp gf garlic granules

Method

- Mix all the ingredients together.
- Divide the mixture into 20 and form each piece into a small ball.
- Fry for 10 minutes, turning frequently.
- Pat the balls dry with kitchen paper to remove excess oil.

Cheat

- *For a very quick and easy version of Italian meatballs, in tomato sauce: use a jar of the Dolmio sauce (see above for details), add to it a packet of Scan Authentic Swedish Meatballs, cook together and serve up with some gf pasta of your choice. A very quick, cheap and easy gf/cf meal that all the family will enjoy.*

Spicy lamb meatballs

These are not suitable for freezing. I admit to being a cumin fan, so although I have already reduced the amount of cumin that I add to this recipe, you may well wish to reduce it again. These needn't be just used for adding to a pasta sauce – they are great on their own, with a salad. Or try either type of meatball as a finger food for a child's party. They make a tasty change from cocktail sausages.

Ingredients

I large onion, grated
I lb minced lamb
1 ½ tsps gf ground cumin
2 cloves garlic, crushed

½ tsp salt
½ tsp fresh ground black pepper
I lemon, juice and grated rind

Method

- Mix together all the ingredients. Cover and refrigerate overnight.
- Divide the mixture into 28 and form into balls.
- Brush each lightly with sunflower oil.
- Grill for 10–15 minutes on a high heat, turning and basting frequently.

Falafels

This recipe makes a good vegetarian alternative to meatballs. Falafels are traditionally served with either pitta bread or couscous, both of which are on the list of forbidden foods now, as they contain gluten. Try using the spicy chickpea pancakes (see Breakfasts for recipe) instead of pitta breads or using quinoa as a couscous substitute.

These also taste great in pasta sauces or with a salad. If you are going to serve them with a pasta sauce then it is best to keep them apart from the sauce, until you are ready to serve them. Prolonged cooking in a sauce tends to make them fall apart.

If you like falafels, but don't want to make them, Just Wholefoods make a good packet-mix version, to which you just add water, oil and lemon juice. Cauldron Foods produce a ready-made falafel. Both are gf/cf, organic, reasonably priced and available in health food shops. If you have problems getting hold of them, refer to the Specialist Suppliers Directory.

Ingredients

14 oz tin chickpeas, drained
I tsp gf ground cumin
I tsp gf ground coriander
I small onion, finely chopped
I tsp gf dried parsley
2 cloves garlic, crushed
I tbsp lemon juice

¼ tsp gf chilli powder/cayenne
    pepper (optional)
I egg, beaten
3 oz gf breadcrumbs
2 oz white rice flour

Method

- Mash the chickpeas roughly with a fork.
- Add the cumin, coriander, onion, parsley, garlic, lemon juice and chilli/cayenne, and mix very well.
- Stir in the egg, breadcrumbs and flour.
- Divide the mixture up and roll into walnut-size pieces.
- Fry for 5 minutes and drain well.

Stews and casseroles

I love stews and casseroles, mainly, I think, because you have only one casserole dish to wash up. They also have the advantage of tasting better the next day. I'm always happy to eat the same thing two days running, as it means even less time in the kitchen. You may well have lots of your own recipes that you will find easy to convert to being gf/cf. If not, here are a few.

Lamb and bean casserole

Makes 4 adult portions.

Ingredients

1½ lb lean lamb, cubed
1 oz white rice flour
14 oz tin chopped tomatoes, drained
2 onions, sliced
½ pint gf/cf vegetable stock (see Lunches, Suppers and Snacks for recipe)

1 tsp gf dried thyme or gf mixed herbs
2 14 oz tins gf/cf baked beans
Sunflower oil

Method

- Coat the lamb in the flour and fry it in sunflower oil until the lamb is brown.
- Add the tomatoes and onions and cook for 2 minutes.
- Add the stock and thyme/mixed herbs and bring the mix up to boiling.
- Reduce the heat to low, cover the pan and simmer for approximately 1 hour or until the lamb is tender.
- Stir in the beans and cook for about a further 5 minutes, to heat the beans through.

Moroccan lamb stew

This is a lovely spicy (but not hot) stew that is great served with plain boiled rice instead of potatoes. If your child eats a wide range of foods, don't write this stew off because of the spices it includes. Prior to Jack's MMR jab, his very favourite food was lamb mince flavoured with lots of garlic and even more cumin. He won't touch it with a barge pole now, but I'm optimistic that one day... So try this with your child and you may well be surprised.

Ingredients

2 onions, chopped
1 lb minced lamb
1 tsp gf ground cinnamon
½ tsp gf allspice

14 oz tin chickpeas
14 oz tin chopped tomatoes
1 lb sweet potatoes, cubed
2 courgettes, sliced

Method

- Gently fry the onions for 3 minutes.
- Add the mince and spices and cook for a further 10 minutes.
- Add the chickpeas, tomatoes and sweet potatoes and simmer for 20 minutes.
- Add the courgettes and simmer for a further 10 minutes.

Mixed lentil casserole

This is a very filling vegetarian casserole. It cannot be frozen. If your child has candida, omit the mushrooms.

Ingredients

½ tsp gf ground cumin
½ tsp gf ground coriander
½ tsp gf mustard powder
½ tsp gf ground ginger
¼ tsp gf turmeric
3 onions, sliced
1 lb carrots, sliced
1 lb leeks, sliced

½ lb turnip, sliced
1 lb button mushrooms, halved
3 tbsps sunflower oil
2 cloves garlic, crushed
6 oz split lentils
2 oz brown or green lentils
1½ pints of boiling water

Method

- In a very large saucepan, heat the oil and fry the onions, carrots, leeks and turnips, for 3 minutes.
- Add the mushrooms, garlic, ginger, turmeric, cumin, coriander and mustard powder and fry for a further 3 minutes.
- Stir in the lentils and the boiling water. Bring the casserole up to boiling.
- Transfer to a casserole dish. Place in the oven and cook for 45–60 minutes at gas mark 4 (180°C/350°F).

Herb dumplings

Nothing finishes a good stew off better than dumplings. My thanks go to Barbara Powell, of Barbara's Kitchen, for this recipe.

Ingredients

1½ oz tapioca starch
1½ oz white rice flour
1½ oz cf margarine
2 tsps gf baking powder

1 tsp xanthan gum
1 pinch salt
½ tsp gf dried mixed herbs
Water

Method

- Gently mix together the flour, starch, salt, baking powder and xanthan gum.
- Mix in the margarine, until the mixture resembles breadcrumbs.
- Mix in the herbs.
- Add sufficient water to produce a soft dough.
- Divide the mixture into 3 and shape into balls.
- Place on top of the stew when it has only 15 minutes left to cook.

Other main meals

Shepherd's pie

This is suitable for freezing. If your child has candida, omit the mushrooms. If your child is allergic to tomatoes, omit these. If your child is all right with tomatoes, you can bulk this meal out even more by adding a large tin of gf/cf baked beans. For vegetarians, omit the mince and use instead gf/cf TVP. Makes 4–5 adult servings.

Ingredients

I large onion, chopped
2 oz button mushrooms, sliced
14 oz tin mixed vegetables
I lb lean minced beef
I bay leaf
2 tbsps white rice flour

I pint gf/cf vegetable or beef stock
I tbsp gf tomato puree
1½ lb potatoes
I oz cf margarine
4 tbsps soya or rice milk

Method

- Gently fry the mince, onions and mushrooms for 10 minutes, stirring frequently.
- Add the flour, stir in well and cook for a further minute.
- Blend in the stock and tomato puree, stirring until it has thickened.
- Add a bay leaf.
- Cover the pan and simmer for 20–25 minutes.
- Cook the potatoes, until ready to mash. Drain and mash with the margarine and milk.
- When the mince mix is ready, stir in tinned vegetables (and baked beans, if adding) and transfer to a 3 pint casserole dish. Remove bay leaf.
- Cover the mince mixture with the mashed potato and bake for 20 minutes at gas mark 6 (200°C/400°F).

Lamb 'shepherd's pie'

This is also suitable for freezing. Makes 4 adult servings.

Ingredients

I lb minced lamb
4 tsps cornflour
2 leeks, sliced
2 large sweet potatoes
2 large onions
I pint gf/cf vegetable stock (see Lunches, Suppers and Snacks for recipe)

14 oz tin mixed vegetables
3 medium parsnips
I tsp gf dried mixed herbs or gf ground cumin
2 oz cf margarine

Method

- In a large pan, brown the minced lamb, then add the onions and cook until they have softened.
- Stir in the cornflour.
- Add seasoning, herbs, leeks and stock and simmer for 20 minutes.
- Cook the parsnip and sweet potato separately, until ready to mash.
- Mash each, mix together and add the margarine and mash again.
- Stir the mixed vegetables into the mince mix.
- Transfer the mince mix to a casserole dish and cover with the mashed parsnips and sweet potatoes.
- Bake for 15 minutes at gas mark 6 (200°C/400°F).

De luxe bubble and squeak

Traditional bubble and squeak is gf/cf, as long as you don't add any fats or oils containing gluten or casein during the cooking process. This recipe however, takes bubble and squeak away from being a side dish and a way of using up leftovers, to make it a meal in itself. It is very quick, very cheap and very filling.

Ingredients

8 oz rindless gf/cf bacon
1 small onion, finely chopped
1 red pepper, finely sliced
Leftover potatoes and cabbage

Method

- Gently fry the bacon. Remove from the oil with a slotted spoon.
- Fry the onion and pepper for 3 minutes.
- Add the potatoes and cabbage, mix together well and cook for a further 10 minutes.
- Add bacon, cook for a further 5–10 minutes until the mixture is very hot and the potatoes are beginning to crisp and brown.

Variation

- I add garlic and cumin to this, but as you've guessed by now, I add these to most things.

Posh bubble cakes

This is a very filling vegetarian 'posh' bubble and squeak that is formed into individual 'cake' servings – hence the name. This makes 6 very large 'cakes'.

Ingredients

5 medium potatoes, peeled, chopped and boiled

½ lb spring greens, washed, drained and shredded

I onion, finely chopped

I leek, finely sliced

I red pepper, finely chopped

2 cloves garlic, crushed

I tsp gf mixed herbs

I tsp gf tomato puree

I egg, beaten

Cornflour or white rice flour, to dust

Method

- Cook potatoes, drain well and allow to cool.
- Lightly cook the spring greens, drain and allow to cool.
- Fry all of the remaining vegetables in a little oil for 2 minutes.
- Add garlic, herbs and tomato puree and continue to fry gently for 5 minutes.
- Remove from the heat and allow to stand for 2 minutes.
- Add the potatoes and greens to the pan and roughly mash and mix together. Allow the mixture to cool completely.
- Sprinkle the cornflour/white rice flour onto a chopping board/baking tray and turn out the mix.
- Divide the mix into 6 and shape into burger shapes that are ½ inch thick. Place mix in freezer for 30 minutes to chill.
- Brush 'cakes' with beaten egg.
- Fry in hot oil for 4 minutes each side. Do not attempt to lift them or move them before this time or they will fall apart.
- Pat off excess oil with kitchen paper. Serve immediately.

Desserts

Desserts can pose a problem when you first try the diet if, like me, you relied heavily upon yoghurts, fromage frais and other milk-based puddings for your child. The Specialist Suppliers Directory, towards the back of the book, will let you know where you can purchase gf/cf yoghurts, ice creams and other desserts.

Ice cream

Please spare a thought for me: I really do not like ice cream (I'm more of a sorbet fan), but I had to make so much ice cream to get this right. I found it very hard to duplicate the extra creamy taste of normal ice cream. Hardly surprising, considering the main ingredient of normal ice cream is cream! However, just before this book went to press, I finally did it. The first recipe is definitely the best. It looks and tastes just like normal ice cream. I have left the recipes for the best of the rest of the ice creams I had tried, as there is no accounting for taste, and you and your child may well prefer one of the others.

If, like me, you thought ice cream is hard to make and time consuming, it isn't. The actual time you spend preparing the ice cream is only about 30 minutes, spread over three separate occasions. The only lengthy bit is the freezing and refreezing, but you have nothing to do with it then. It is even easier if you invest in an ice-cream maker. I did this recently and it is well worth it for the difference it makes and the time it saves.

Both recipes for vanilla ice-cream go really well with the chocolate fudge sauce recipe (see below).

The best gf/cf vanilla ice cream

Ingredients

¾ pint gf/cf single cream (e.g. Provamel soya cream alternative)

¾ pint gf/cf plain yoghurt (e.g. Provamel plain organic yofu)

6 oz caster sugar

2 tsps gf vanilla extract

Method

- Over a very low heat, melt the sugar into the cream. When the sugar has dissolved, remove the mixture from the heat and allow to cool.

- Whisk in the yoghurt and the vanilla extract.

Then either:

- Churn as normal in an ice-cream maker for 30 minutes.

Or:

- Pour into a freezer-proof container.

- When cold, place in freezer for approximately 3 hours.

- Remove from freezer and with a fork, mash the mixture to break up the ice crystals.

- Freeze again for approximately 2 hours.

- Remove and remash.

- Freeze for approximately 3 hours.

- Remove from freezer 20 minutes before you are ready to serve it, to soften.

Vanilla ice cream or lolly mix

You can either use this to make ice cream or pour the mix into ice-lolly moulds to make a milk-flavoured lolly, which is what the taste of this recipe resembles.

Ingredients

1 pint soya or rice milk
2 tsps gf vanilla extract
4 egg yolks, beaten

4 oz caster sugar
3 tbsps sunflower oil

Method

- Mix the sugar and egg yolks together well.
- Stir in the milk, oil and vanilla extract.
- Strain the mixture into a heavy-based saucepan.
- Cook the mix over a very gentle heat, stirring all the time, until it is just thick enough to begin to coat the spoon as you are stirring.
- Be careful not to overheat the mixture, as it will curdle.
- Either allow to cool and churn in ice-cream maker for 30 minutes or follow the instructions below for making ice cream by hand.
- Remove from heat; pour into a freezer-proof container.
- When cold, place in freezer for approximately 3 hours.
- Remove from freezer and with a fork, mash the mixture to break up the ice crystals.
- Freeze again for approximately 2 hours.
- Remove and remash.
- Freeze for approximately 3 hours.
- Remove from freezer 20 minutes before you are ready to serve it, to soften.

Variations

- *Fruit: add ½ pint of cooked, cooled fruit puree to the ice-cream mix before its first trip to the freezer.*
- *Chocolate: melt 2oz of plain gf/cf chocolate, allow to cool and add to mix just prior to removing from heat. Stir in well.*

Soya yoghurt ice cream

Ingredients

7 fl oz soya milk
2 egg yolks, beaten
1 cup caster sugar

17 fl oz plain gf/cf soya yoghurt
2 tsps gf/cf vanilla extract

Method

- Combine together the egg yolks and sugar.
- Heat the milk until it boils, remove from heat and stir in the egg mix.
- Return to a low heat and gently heat through, stirring continuously, until the mix coats the back of the spoon with a fine film.
- Remove from heat and allow to cool.
- Mix in the yoghurt and vanilla extract, then follow the steps above for making ice cream by hand.

Variations

As for vanilla ice cream.

Banana and honey tofu ice cream

This is a creamier ice cream than the recipe above and it has the added benefit of having extra protein from the tofu. Tofu is really easy to get hold of; nearly all supermarkets stock it, in their chill cabinets. It is also egg free, in case your child has an egg allergy. But it goes without saying that this recipe is completely out of the question if your child has a soya or a banana allergy.

Unless the tofu is very well blended, the ice cream can have a granular texture. It is worth getting the food processor out to blend down the tofu, rather than trying to do it by hand.

It is very quick to make. It only takes 10 minutes of your time, in between its trips to the freezer.

This recipe gets Luke's seal of approval. Jack has an intolerance to bananas.

Ingredients

250 g tofu
200 ml soya or rice milk
3–4 bananas, roughly sliced

100 g honey
½ tsp gf vanilla extract

Method

- Place all the ingredients in a blender and mix until smooth and creamy.
- Pour into a freezer-proof container and freeze for 3 hours.
- Remove and either mash out ice crystals with a fork or put back into the blender to remove crystals.
- Refreeze for 2 hours and repeat mashing.
- Refreeze for 3 hours.
- Remove from freezer 20 minutes before serving, to allow to soften.
- Alternatively, use an ice-cream maker and follow the instructions for ordinary ice cream.

Sorbets

In my opinion sorbets beat ice creams hands down, and I was only too happy to try all the varieties. All the sorbets need a basic sugar syrup solution.

Sorbet sugar syrup

Makes 12 fl oz.

Ingredients

4 oz granulated sugar   ½ pint water

Method

- In a heavy-based saucepan, gently heat the water and sugar until the sugar dissolves.
- Once all the sugar has dissolved, bring to the boil and continue to boil for 2 minutes.
- Allow to cool before using.

Lemon sorbet

Ingredients

12 fl oz sugar syrup
3 lemons, rind and juice

1 egg white

Method

- Add the lemon rind to the sugar and water before bringing it to the boil and simmer gently for 10 minutes. Then boil the syrup for a further 2 minutes.
- Allow the syrup to cool completely, then strain off the rind.
- Stir in lemon juice.
- Place in shallow freezer-proof container. Cover and freeze for approximately 3 hours, until 'mushy'.
- Whisk egg white until very stiff.
- Turn out sorbet into a bowl and break down ice crystals gently with back of a metal fork.
- Gently fold in egg white.
- Return to container, cover and freeze for a further 4 hours.
- Allow to soften slightly before serving.

Strawberry sorbet

Ingredients

12 fl oz sugar syrup
1 lb strawberries

2 tbsps lemon juice
2 egg whites

Method

- Puree the strawberries in a blender and then strain through a sieve.
- Mix the strawberry puree with the sugar syrup and lemon juice.
- Place in shallow freezer-proof container. Cover and freeze for approximately 3 hours, until 'mushy'.
- Whisk egg white until very stiff.
- Turn out sorbet into a bowl and break down ice crystals gently with back of a metal fork.

- Gently fold in egg white.
- Return to container, cover and freeze for a further 4 hours.
- Allow to soften slightly before serving.

Other desserts

Chocolate pudding

This is a very thick, rich and creamy pudding. If you wish to increase the chocolate content, remember to increase the sugar too, otherwise you will have an overpowering flavour of chocolate, with a very bitter aftertaste.

This also works well as an ice-cream mix. Follow the method for the banana and honey tofu ice cream above.

Ingredients
9 oz gf/cf tofu
½ pint soya or rice milk

2 oz caster sugar
2–3 oz gf/cf chocolate

Method

- Blend the tofu and ¼ pint of milk together, in an electric blender.
- Over a low heat, melt the sugar and chocolate into the remaining ¼ pint of milk.
- Allow the chocolate mix to cool and then blend into the tofu mix.
- Cool in an airtight container in the fridge for 2–3 hours or until set.

Baked banana boats

This recipe is so easy and quick, not to mention delicious and cheap.

Ingredients
4 ripe bananas
1 oz cf margarine

1 tbsp caster sugar

Method

- Leaving the bananas in their skins, cut deep slits lengthways down the bananas, but not deep enough to cut right through.
- Open bananas slightly.
- Cream together the margarine and the sugar.
- Divide the margarine and sugar mix into 4 and push it down into each banana. Then press the banana back together again.
- Place the bananas in a microwaveable dish, slit side up, and bake on high power for 3–4 minutes, when the skins should begin to blacken. The banana will be soft and beginning to become translucent.
- Serve immediately, leaving the bananas still in their skins.

*** **Warning** *** Do not overfill the bananas. If you do, the skins will split open during cooking, depositing this delicious concoction all over the inside of your microwave.

Variations

- *Omit the margarine and sugar mix and substitute lemon and sugar, honey or gf/cf chocolate (what child could resist this?) or chocolate fudge sauce (see below for recipe).*

Chinese banana fritters

This is a little bit fiddly when compared to the baked bananas (above), but well worth the extra few minutes it takes.

Ingredients

4 bananas
1 egg, beaten
Bowl of ice-cold water
4 tbsps cornflour

4 oz caster sugar
1 tbsp sesame seeds
3 tbsps sunflower oil and more for frying

Method

- Cut the bananas in half lengthways and then cut each piece into 4 widthways.
- Blend the egg and cornflour together until you have a smooth paste.
- Add just enough of the ice-cold water to turn the paste into a batter.

- Heat enough oil in a wok to cover the bananas (or set your deep fat fryer to 180°C/350°F).
- Dip each piece of banana in the batter and deep fry for 2–3 minutes.
- Drain off the excess oil from the banana and pat dry with kitchen paper.
- In a heavy-based pan, heat the sugar and 3 tbsps of oil on a low heat for 5 minutes.
- Carefully add 3 tbsps of water to the sugar mix and stir for 2 minutes.
- Stir in the sesame seeds.
- Add the banana fritters and stir slowly and gently, until all the fritters are covered in the sugar solution.
- As soon as the sugar solution begins to caramelise, remove from heat and take out the fritters and plunge them straight into a bowl of ice-cold water to harden.

Meringues

Ingredients
3 egg whites
6 oz caster sugar

Method

- Whisk the egg whites, either by hand or with an electric mixer on the lowest setting, until the mixture is very stiff and will stand up in peaks.
- Fold in the sugar a little at a time, with a metal spoon.
- Using a piping bag, pipe the mixture into the required shape and size, onto a baking tray lined with greaseproof paper. As I do not own a piping bag, I just spoon the mixture onto the tray. Not very professional looking, but it does the job.
- Bake at gas mark ¼ (110°C/225°F) for 2 hours until they are well dried out.
- Remove from tray and cool on a wire rack.

Eat on their own or sandwich two together with a little jam or pureed fruit.

Pear meringue pie

Ingredients

8 oz gf/cf pastry (see recipe in Odds and Ends)
1 lb stewed and pureed pears, cooled
Meringue mix (as above)

Method

- Line a 9-inch sandwich tin with greaseproof paper.
- Roll out the pastry and line the tin with it. Allow it to cool in the fridge for 30–60 minutes.
- Bake blind at gas mark 5 (190°C/375°F) for approximately 20 minutes, until cooked and pale brown.
- Spread the pear puree over the pastry.
- Spoon the meringue mix on top and pull it up into small peaks with a knife.
- Bake at gas mark 5 (190°C/375°F) for 5–10 minutes until the meringue is light brown on the peaks.
- Allow to cool before serving.

Lemon meringue pie

Ingredients

8 oz gf/cf pastry (see Odds and Ends)   2½ oz cornflour
Meringue mix (see above)   3 oz caster sugar
2 lemons, juice and grated rinds   3 egg yolks, beaten
1 pint cold water

Method

- Prepare the pastry case as for pear meringue.
- To make the lemon filling, place the lemon rinds and 1 pint of cold water in a saucepan.
- Bring to the boil. Remove from heat and allow to stand for 30 minutes.
- Add the lemon juice.

- Take out 4 tbsps of lemon water and mix it with the cornflour, to form a smooth paste.
- Add the paste to the lemon water and stir well.
- Bring the mix back to the boil, stirring constantly.
- Reduce the heat and cook until thickened. Stir constantly.
- Remove from heat and stir in the sugar.
- Add egg yolks and stir vigorously, until well mixed.
- Pour into the pastry case.
- Cover with meringue and bake as for pear meringue.

Custard

Thanks go to my mum for this recipe. It is a lovely custard, much better than packet custard. But the good news for those of us who want to spend as little time in the kitchen as possible is that many custard powders are gf/cf, as well as being egg free. All you do is substitute soya or rice milk during cooking.

Instant custard powder, flavoured custard and ready-made custards are definitely not gf/cf.

Ingredients

½ pint soya milk
1 tbsp cornflour
1 tsp gf vanilla extract

1 egg, beaten
½–1 tbsp caster sugar (depending upon taste)

Method

- Mix together in a heatproof bowl the egg, cornflour, sugar and vanilla with a little of the milk, to form a smooth, creamy paste.
- Heat the remainder of the milk, until it almost reaches boiling point.
- Pour the milk into the paste and stir constantly.
- Return the custard to the saucepan and reheat, until the custard thickens.
- Serve immediately.

Variations

- *Chocolate custard – add 1 tbsp of gf/cf cocoa powder to the egg, cornflour and vanilla, at the beginning of the recipe.*
- *Banana custard – add 2 chopped bananas when the custard has thickened. Serve hot or chill in the fridge.*

Chocolate fudge sauce

This is a versatile sauce that can be used either as an ice-cream sauce or, by reducing the milk down to 2 tbsps, as a cake covering/filling.

Ingredients

5 tbsps rice or soya milk
1 oz gf/cf cocoa powder
4 oz caster sugar

6 oz golden syrup
1 oz cf margarine
½ tsp gf vanilla extract

Method

- Mix together all the ingredients (except the vanilla), in a saucepan, over a low heat.
- Slowly bring the mixture up to boiling point, stirring occasionally.
- Boil for 5 minutes.
- Add the vanilla and stir well.
- Remove from heat and allow to cool slightly before serving.

Odds and Ends

This is a selection of gf/cf recipes that I could not fit into the above categories.

Pastry

I've left this recipe to the end, because now I have to admit that this one was almost beyond me. I can just about make normal shortcrust pastry, but gave up quickly when I found out you could get frozen pastry. This recipe does work, it tastes and looks fine, but I did find the pastry difficult to roll out and move about. Whatever you do, make sure that you line the cooking container with greaseproof paper, unless you are doing jam tarts or something of a similar size – then just grease the container well. Gluten Free Pantry do a good packet mix for pastry (available via mail order from Gourmet Gluten Free Imports – see Specialist Suppliers Directory). It is a sweet pastry; great for jam tarts and meringue pies. This was the very first pastry Jack ever ate. If you need a pastry for a savoury dish, then the following recipe is for you (Nutrition Point's White Mix also makes a very good pastry). This recipe can also be used for sweet recipes. The secret of pastry making is to keep everything as cold as possible, for as long as possible.

Ingredients

1 ¼ cups gf flour mix
1 tsp salt
⅔ cup cold cf margarine or ⅓ cup cf margarine
   and ⅓ cup lard, chopped into small cubes

¼ cup iced water
White rice flour for
   dusting rolling surface

Method

- Mix together the flour and salt.
- Rub in the fat, with your fingertips, until it resembles fine breadcrumbs.
- Slowly add the water (you may not need it all), until the mix binds together.

- Chill the pastry in the fridge for at least an hour.
- Roll out to the required shape; you will have to use a lot of white rice flour on your rolling surface.
- Line your tin with greaseproof paper.
- If you have time, chill the pastry again before cooking.

Mayonnaise

There are several gf/cf mayonnaises on the market, the most well known and easy to obtain being Hellmann's Real Mayonnaise (the original) or their Mediterranean version. But having now mastered gf/cf cooking, something as simple as mayonnaise will hold no fear for you.

This mayonnaise will keep for up to three days, stored in the fridge in an airtight container.

Ingredients

I egg yolk, at room
  temperature
½ tsp gf mustard powder
½ tsp salt

¼ tsp fresh ground black pepper
I tbsp gf white wine vinegar or lemon
  juice
¼ pint sunflower oil

Method

- Mix together the egg yolk, mustard powder, seasoning and I tsp of the vinegar/lemon juice.
- Add the oil, little by little, continuously whisking, until the mixture becomes thick and smooth.
- Slowly add the remaining vinegar/lemon juice and mix well.

Sage and onion stuffing

This recipe makes enough to stuff a large chicken. It's incredibly easy to do and costs very little. If that has not convinced you to have a go, both Allergyfree Direct and Allergycare have a suitable stuffing mix (the Allergycare one is also yeast and egg free). See Specialist Suppliers Directory for details.

If your child does have an egg allergy, increase the margarine to 2 oz and bind the mixture together with a very little cf milk or water.

Ingredients

1 large onion, finely chopped
1 oz cf margarine
2 tbsps fresh sage, chopped or 1 ½ tsps gf dried sage

2 oz gf breadcrumbs
Zest of ¼ lemon, finely grated
½ beaten egg

Method

- Gently fry onion in the margarine until soft.
- Add sage, breadcrumbs, lemon zest and egg. Mix them in well.
- Allow to go cold before stuffing the bird.

Chicken liver pâté

I always get stuck for sandwich fillings for Jack. Apart from the things that are restricted by the diet, he restricts so much more himself. Although he is not at the stage (yet) to accept this, I adapted a mild, smooth pâté recipe that I've used for years and particularly like. I hope that by the time you are reading this, Jack and I will be tucking into this pâté.

It is possible to get gf/cf pâtés from supermarket own ranges (check individual supermarkets' lists) and also to get a range of pâtés from specialist suppliers (see Directory).

Ingredients

1 onion, finely chopped
2 oz cf margarine
1 lb chicken livers, chopped
1 garlic clove, finely chopped

½ tsp gf dried mixed herbs
1 tsp lemon juice
Salt and fresh ground black pepper to taste

Method

- Melt the margarine in a pan and gently sauté the onions.
- Add the chicken livers, herbs and garlic and cook on a moderate heat for 10 minutes, stirring occasionally.
- Remove the pan from heat and stir in the lemon.
- Allow the mixture to cool and place in a blender. Blend until it is a smooth consistency.
- Stir in the required seasoning.
- Chill for a minimum of 2 hours before use.

If your child rejects the pâté, don't throw it away; add a couple of teaspoons (or more) of brandy and you will have a really tasty adult pâté.

Pesto

I love pesto, but one of its main ingredients is parmesan cheese, so it's obviously not gf/cf. This recipe works just as well in any pasta dishes that require pesto. It's super-quick to make and will store for up to three weeks in the fridge in an airtight container.

If you are determined to make an authentic pesto, it is possible to get a parmesan substitute (see Specialist Suppliers Directory for details).

Ingredients

2 oz fresh basil leaves, roughly chopped.
2 garlic cloves, crushed

2 tbsps pine nuts
4 fl oz gf olive oil

Method

- Place all the ingredients in a blender and blend at high speed, until the mixture is very creamy.

GF Play dough

This is probably the most important recipe in the book, after the chicken nuggets! There are loads of different recipes around, but I've found this one to be the most robust.

I was absolutely heartbroken when I found out that commercial play doughs contained approximately 40 per cent gluten, because I had spent months with Jack, before he went to nursery and playgroup, working through his tactical defensiveness to get him to touch the stuff. Once I had succeeded, he used to clamour daily to play with it.

I suggest that you make a big batch of this and send some along to your child's class/playgroup/nursery. I am really pleased by the support that Jack's nursery has given me with the diet, to the extent that they threw away all their play dough and use the gf version for all the children. This was especially important for me, as Jack's first dietary infringement happened at playgroup, when he managed to move faster than me and eat a fingernailful of play dough. He couldn't go back there for a week and he and I didn't get much sleep for the next few days.

Like all home-made play doughs, it needs to be stored in an airtight container. There is no need to store it in the fridge. When you are ready to use it, you will notice that it has taken on a 'crusty' appearance. This is only the salt crystallising on the surface. To get it ready for your child to play with, just work it through your hands a few times.

It goes without saying that like every other recipe here, it is very simple to make.

Ingredients

½ cup of rice flour 2 tsps cream of tartar
½ cup maize meal flour 1 cup water
½ cup salt   1 tsp sunflower oil

Method

- Combine all the ingredients in a heavy-based saucepan.

- Cook over a low heat and stir very occasionally.

- When it combines together to form one ball/lump, remove from heat and allow to cool.

- When it is cool enough to touch, work it through with your hands a few times, before storing in an airtight container.

Specialist Suppliers
and Mail Order Directory

All details are correct at the time of going to press. The author and publisher accept no liability for any changes made to products, ingredients and the manufacturing process. It is the responsibility of the individual to check details prior to use.

This is in no way a complete list of specialist suppliers – that would be another book entirely! Inclusion (or omission) from this directory does not constitute approval (or disapproval) of the company and its products.

Allergycare Ltd

1 Church Square
Taunton
Somerset
TA1 1SA
Tel: 01823 625022
Fax: 01823 325024

This company also has a nutritional helpline available at the telephone number listed above. They are a well-known company and many of their products, some of which are suitable for the gf/cf diet, are available in health food shops and via the other distributors listed here. You can order direct from Allergycare. Products that are suitable for the diet include:

- Soya milk powder
- Milkshake powder (soya based)
- Stuffing mix (yeast and egg free)
- Baking powder
- Whizzers chocolate beans (colourful, but contain no artificial colours or preservatives. Contain soya lecithin. Similar to a well-known sweet brand)
- Carob bars (sugar free, contain soya)
- Versaloaf (add to water and gf flour of choice to make gf/cf and yeast free bread)

- Organic gf flours (buckwheat, tapioca, sago, brown rice, millet)

Allergyfree Direct Ltd
5 Centremead
Osney Mead
Oxfordshire
OX2 0ES
Tel: 01865 722003
Fax: 01865 244134
Web: www.allergyfreedirect.co.uk

This company supply a wide variety of products. Some are gf/cf, some are not. They also stock a wide range of organic products. Telephone for a free product catalogue. The following list will give you an idea of the wide range of products supplied that are gf/cf:

- Baking powder
- Chocolate
- Rice milk powder
- Soya milk powder
- Milkshake powders
- Breads (contain yeast)
- Veggie burger mix
- Pretzels
- Stuffing mix
- Pakora mix
- Organic fruit spreads
- Canned spaghetti (in tomato sauce)
- Biscuits
- Pâtés, dips and spreads
- Yoghurts (some contain apple juice)
- Veggie sausage mix
- Pastas and noodles
- Sourdough breads (yeast free)
- Pasta sauces
- Puffed rice cereal
- Imagine puddings (rice syrup based)
- Veggie ready meals
- Parmazano (soya-based parmesan-style seasoning)

- ∘ Crackers
- ∘ Crispbreads
- ∘ Soups
- ∘ Beans and pulses

Alternative Cakes

Unit 8C
Amble Industrial Estate
Amble
Northumberland
NE65 0PE
Tel/fax: 01665 712360
Web: www.alternativecakes.com
Email: info@alternativecakes.com

This company produce hand-made traditional cakes. All products are free from MSG, aspartame and genetically modified ingredients. All the eggs used are free-range and all products are suitable for vegetarians. Some of their extensive range is gluten free and this gluten free range is produced in a separate environment from the gluten-containing cakes, to prevent cross-contamination. They also produce two gf/cf loaves that are yeast free.

The cakes and bread are available at selected health food stores or you can order direct from the company by phone or via the Internet.

Probably the best news of all is that they are able to supply direct to you (rather than through shops) gf/cf, additive free and vegan chocolate cake, coffee cake, lemon cake, cherry cake and carrot cake. All of these cakes contain soya flour. They are also happy to make gf/cf birthday cakes, which are either chocolate or vanilla flavoured.

They have asked me to point out that they are able to accommodate many other food allergies in creating their cakes; all you have to do is ask. Of their standard gluten free range, the following are also casein free:

- ∘ Iced gluten free celebration cake – a rich fruit cake, covered in gluten free marzipan and icing. Contains soya.
- ∘ Gluten free celebration cake – as above, without the icing and marzipan. Contains soya.
- ∘ Just fruit cake – contains soya

- White sandwich loaf – yeast free, contains soya
- Brown sandwich loaf – yeast free, contains soya

Barbara's Kitchen

PO Box 54
Pontyclun
South Wales
CF72 8WD
Tel/Fax: 01443 229304
Web: www.barbaraskitchen.co.uk
Email: enquiries@barbaraskitchen.co.uk

A few of Barbara's recipes have appeared in this book. She has more! She will also adapt them if your child has other intolerances. Barbara has many food intolerances herself and she knows that the difference between delicious gf/cf baking and something fit only for the birds to eat is as much to do with using good-quality ingredients, as having a good recipe. She can supply you with:

- Xanthan gum (vital if you are going to bake with gf flour)
- White rice flour
- Potato starch flour (farina)
- Tapioca starch flour (cassava)
- Set of four USA measuring cups (recommended for accurately following recipes)
- Set of measuring spoons

Barbara also does a 'starter pack' of the above.

Barkat (see Gluten free foods)

Bi-Aglut

Novartis Consumer Health
Wimblehurst Road
Horsham
West Sussex
RH12 5AB
Tel: 0845 601 2665 (lo-call)
Web: www.biaglut.co.uk

This company produce a small range of gluten free foods, all of which are available on prescription. The following are also casein free, egg free and free from genetically modified ingredients, but all contain soya:

- Cracker toasts (fette tostate)
- Crackers
- Penne
- Spaghetti
- Fusilli
- Macaroni

Big Oz

PO Box 48
Twickenham
Middlesex
TW1 2UF
Tel: 01895 445896
Web: www.bigoz.co.uk

This company import a range of organic breakfast cereals from Australia (hence the name). All the cereals are free from sugar, artificial sweeteners, colouring, flavourings, preservatives and yeast and have a shelf-life of 18 months. The products need to be ordered direct from the company. Of the range, four of the cereals are suitable for the diet:

- Buckwheat Puffs
- Corn Puffs
- Millet Puffs
- Rice Puffs

Brewhurst Health Food Supplies Ltd

Abbot Close
Oyster Lane
Byfleet
Surrey
KT14 7JP
Tel: 01932 334501
Fax: 01932 336235
Web: www.brewhurst.com
Email: info@brewhurst.com

This company supply a variety of products that are gf; many are cf too. They also supply gf/cf cheese! These products should be available from your local health food store. Some of the products that are suitable for the gf/cf diet are:

- Muesli (egg and soya free)
- Cakes
- Bread mix
- Cake mix
- Pasta (both rice and corn varieties, egg and soya free)
- Ready-made breads
- Cheese slices (cheddar and mozzarella style, soya based)
- Cookies

Cauldron Foods Ltd

Units 1–2
Portishead Business Park
Portishead
Bristol
BS20 7BF
Tel: 01275 818448
Fax: 01275 818353
Web: www.cauldronfoods.co.uk

This company produce vegetarian, vegan and some organic foods. The soya beans they use for their tofu products are not genetically modified. Most health food stores and some supermarket chains carry at least part of the range. Some of the range is gf/cf, including:

- Tofu (original and smoked)
- Pâtés
- Falafel

Clearspring Ltd

Unit 19A
Acton Park Estate
London
W3 7QE
Tel: 020 8749 1781

Fax: 020 8811 8893
Web: www.clearspring.co.uk
Email: info@clearspring.co.uk

You can find some of these products in some health food stores, but you can also order direct from the company. They deal exclusively with organic and macrobiotic foods imported from Japan. So why do they get listed here? Simply because all their foods are cf, sugar free, GM free, vegetarian, and free from artificial and refined ingredients. On top of that, a lot of their foods are gf too, which is hardly surprising when you think that rice is a staple part of the Japanese diet. Well worth phoning for a copy of their catalogue.

To give you an idea of some of the gf/cf foods, they stock:

- Wafers
- Crackers
- Pulses, seeds, grains
- Pasta (some unusual varieties)
- Noodles (very unusual varieties)
- Dried sea vegetables
- Tofu
- Imagine pudding range (egg and soya free, rice based, four flavours)
- Quinoa
- Fruit purees
- Fruit spreads

D & D Chocolates

261 Forest Road
Loughborough
LE11 3HT
Tel: 01509 216400
Fax: 01509 233961

The entire range of chocolates is gf/cf. They do two varieties, dark couverture chocolate and carob confectionery. They have a wide selection of products and also produce seasonal ranges, such as Christmas novelties to decorate the Christmas tree and Easter eggs. The chocolate may contain traces of nut. Phone for a brochure of their range – happy drooling!

Doves Farm Foods Ltd

Salisbury Road
Hungerford
Berkshire
RG17 0RF
Tel: 01488 684880
Fax: 01488 685235
Web: www.dovesfarm.co.uk
Email: mail@dovesfarm.co.uk

This company supply a range of gluten free goods, but only some of their flours are suitable for gf/cf baking. This is a well-known brand and readily available in most health food shops; many supermarkets are beginning to stock some of the range. The foods that are suitable for the gf/cf diet are:

- Gluten free flour
- Brown rice flour
- Buckwheat flour
- Gram flour
- Maize flour

Everfresh

Gatehouse Close
Aylesbury
Buckinghamshire
HP19 3DE
Tel: 01296 425333
Fax: 01296 422545

This company provide a whole range of products that are cf. Unfortunately, only five of their breads are also gf. But every cloud has a silver lining, as these breads do not contain yeast or any added sugar, and they are also organic. The five breads are:

- Corn rice flax bread
- Corn rice sesame bread
- Corn rice sunflower bread
- Mixed grain gluten free bread
- Spicy onion gluten free bread

Gamble & Hollis

14 Town Square
Syston
Leicester
Tel: 0116 260 3300

This company make a range of gf/cf burgers and sausages, which they will deliver. The range includes:

- Burgers – pork, beef and lamb
- Sausages – pork, lincoln, pork and apple, and pork and chive

General Dietary Ltd

PO Box 38
Kingston upon Thames
Surrey
KT2 7YP
Tel: 020 8336 2323
Fax: 020 8942 8274

General Dietary supply a number of different products from the Ener-G, Valpiform and Tinkyada ranges. The products are only available by mail order from the company. Most of the range is suitable for this diet.

The following breads in the Ener-G range are all prescribable, and sweetened with pear juice (except the rice loaf). The brown rice bread, tapioca bread and white rice bread have added vitamin B1, B2, niacin and iron.

- Brown rice bread (egg and soya free)
- Tapioca bread (egg and soya free)
- White rice bread (egg and soya free)
- Brown rice and maize bread (egg, soya and yeast free, contains almond meal)
- Rice loaf (egg and yeast free)
- Rice pasta (eight types)
- Brown rice pasta (ten types)
- Pure rice bran
- Egg replacer

Glutafin
See entry for **Nutricia**.

Glutano
See entry for **Gluten Free Foods Ltd**.

Gluten Free Foods Ltd
Unit 270 Centennial Park
Centennial Avenue
Elstree
Borehamwood
Herts
WD6 3SS
Tel: 020 8953 4444
Fax: 020 8953 8285
Web: www.glutenfree-foods.co.uk
Email: info@glutenfree-foods.co.uk

All of this company's range of foods is gf. Most of the range is cf too. Their products are readily available in health food stores. Large Tescos are stocking most of the Glutano range. The gf/cf range includes:

- Bread (ready-made and part-baked)
- Rolls
- Pasta
- Biscuits
- Pretzels
- Muesli
- Wafers
- Pizza bases (rice based)

Goodness Direct
PO Box 6049
Daventry
Northamptonshire
NN11 4UY
Tel: 01327 871655
Fax: 01327 310528
Web: www.goodnessdirect.co.uk
Email: info@goodnessdirect.co.uk

This company is an on-line health food shop. They stock a variety of products and the good news is that they have two special sections that cover dairy and gluten free products. They have a wide range of gf/cf foods. As they are continually updating and expanding their product range, I have not listed any of their products here, but they are well worth a look.

Gourmet Gluten-free Imports Ltd
12 Singleton Gardens
Clanfield
Hampshire
PO8 0XN
Tel: 02392 647572
Fax: 02392 431606
Email: info@ggfi.co.uk

Judith and Peter Rodgers import the Gluten Free Pantry range of mixes from America. Judith is intolerant to gluten and set out to find some good alternatives – she has succeeded!

There are 13 mixes in the range, ten of which are gf/cf. All are soya and egg free, except the 'luscious angel food cake' mix, which contains powdered egg whites and the choc chip cookie mix, which contains soya lecithin.

Care is needed when following the recipes on each packet, as they are not designed for a cf diet. Just use cf margarine instead of the butter stated and rice or soya milk instead of cow's milk. So good are these mixes that I have even managed successfully to use soya milk when the recipe has stated using buttermilk.

This company have recently extended their range of products to cover other gf/cf basics outside the Gluten Free Pantry range, but they recommend phoning first to check the availability of these goods before ordering.

The Gluten Free Pantry range of mixes that are gf/cf are:

- Country french bread/pizza mix (contains yeast)
- Tapioca bread mix (contains yeast)
- Old fashioned cake and cookie mix
- Muffins and quick breads mix

- Chocolate truffle brownie mix
- Perfect piecrust mix (a sweet pastry mix, not suitable for savoury fillings)
- Luscious angel food cake mix (contains powdered egg whites)
- Choc chip cookie/squares mix (contains soya lecithin)
- Cranberry orange bread/muffin mix (contains grated orange peel)
- Spice cake and gingerbread mix

Other products available:

- Xanthan gum
- Guar gum (can be used in place of xanthan gum)
- Potato starch
- Tapioca flour
- Vance's dari free (milk alternative)
- Kingsmill vegetarian egg replacer

Innovative Solutions

Cenargo International Freight Terminal
Clayton Road
Hayes
Middlesex
UB3 1AX
Tel/Fax: 020 8756 3820
Email: info@innovative-solutions.org.uk

This company offer a range of gf/cf baking basics, which includes:

- Xanthan gum
- White rice flour
- Brown rice flour
- Tapioca flour
- Potato flour
- Gluten free flour (a premixed flour combining the four flours above)
- Vanilla flavouring (alcohol free)
- Almond flavouring (alcohol free)
- Lemon flavouring (alcohol free)

Just Wholefoods

Unit 16 Cirencester Business Estate
Elliott Road
Love Lane Industrial Estate
Cirencester
Gloucestershire
GL7 1YS
Tel: 01285 651910
Web: www.justwholefoods@demon.co.uk

This company supply a range of vegetarian dried foods which are all free of genetically modified ingredients. Much of their range is also certified organic. Their products are available in good health food shops. All the range is very competitively priced.

They do a range of instant 'make in a cup' soup mixes, some of which are gf/cf. These soups are good on their own but they are also good to use as a tasty stock. Their gf/cf range includes:

- ° Custard powder
- ° Jellies – four varieties
- ° Falafel mix
- ° Pillau mix
- ° Hummus mix
- ° Instant soup mixes – four of which are gf/cf: vegetable, carrot and coriander, leek and potato, and tomato

Lifestyle Healthcare Ltd

Centenary Business Park
Henley-on-Thames
Oxfordshire
RG9 1DS
Tel: 01491 411767
Fax: 01491 571704
Web: www.glutenfree.co.uk

This company do something very special: many of their products are baked to order and despatched the same day! Their fresh produce can be frozen for up to three months. All the fresh-baked foods are soya free. I was pleasantly surprised by the prices too. Many items are considerably cheaper than the 'long life' versions. Their gf/cf fresh baked foods, which are suitable for the gf/cf diet, are:

- Unsliced bread (contains yeast, egg free, prescribable)
- Pizza bases (contain yeast, egg free, prescribable)
- Mini rolls (contain yeast, egg free, prescribable)
- Lemon biscuits
- Orange and chocolate chip cookies
- Peanut butter cookies
- Ginger snaps
- Chocolate chip cookies
- Double chocolate chip cookies
- Pecan and honey biscuits
- Lemon muffins
- Vanilla muffins

This company also do a range of gf/cf foods which can be stored for up to six months without freezing All the products listed below are prescribable. All are egg free except the pizza bases.

- Gf flour (soya free)
- Crackers
- Pasta
- Biscuits
- High fibre bread (contains soya and yeast)
- Pizza bases (contain egg)

Lock's Sausages

West Lane
Edwinstowe
Mansfield
Nottinghamshire
Tel/fax: 01623 822200

Strangely enough, this company make gf/cf sausages (they also do burgers). Orders will be delivered the next day. Their range includes:

- Burgers – beef and pork with apple
- Sausages – pork, pork and chive, pork and apple, and low fat pork

Nutricia Dietary Care
Newland Avenue
White Horse Business Park
Trowbridge
Wiltshire
BA14 0XQ
Tel: 01225 711801
Fax: 01225 711567
Web: www.glutafin.co.uk.
Email: glutenfree@nutricia.co.uk

This company only produce food that is gf; some of the range is cf too.
Much of their range is prescribable. They have two trade name ranges:
Glutafin (ready-made products) and Trufree (a range of flours). All Trufree
flours are gf/cf (all contain soya, most have added vitamins and calcium).
Phone for a full list of their products. The Glutafin gf/cf range includes:

- White flour mix
- Fibre mix
- Multigrain flour mix
- Multigrain fibre mix
- Range of six pastas
- Crackers
- Biscuits and cookies
- Cakes
- Christmas pudding
- Baking powder

Nutrition Point Ltd
13 Taurus Park
Westbrook
Warrington
Cheshire
WA5 5ZT
Tel: 07041 544044 (lo-call rate)
Fax: 07041 544055
Email: info@nutrionpoint.ltd.uk

This company supply 13 gf/cf packet mixes under the name Dietary Specialities, which are imported from America. All packets require only water, and/or oil and sometimes an egg, to make up. All the range are very easy and quick to make. Trust me, you will need absolutely no cookery skills to get these right. All the products are also egg free. Some of the recipes do require an egg to make, but egg replacement powder can be used instead, if necessary. Six of the mixes are available on prescription. The other seven are available by mail order direct from the company. The chocolate cake mix comes highly recommended and is, in my opinion, far too good for children!

Available on prescription:

- White bread mix (soya free, contains yeast)
- Brown bread mix (soya free, contains yeast)
- Fibre mix (soya free)
- Corn bread mix
- White cake mix
- White mix (plain flour mix, soya free)

Available by mail order:

- Chocolate cake mix
- Scotch pancake mix
- Bran muffin mix
- Banana bread mix (contains dried banana pieces)
- Brownie mix (soya free)
- Blueberry muffin mix (no fruit pieces, only flavouring)
- Apple bread mix (contains apple)

The Organic Shop (Online) Ltd

Central Chambers
London Road
Alderley Edge
Cheshire
SK9 7DZ
Tel: 0845 674 4000
Fax: 0845 674 1000
Email: enquiries@theorganicshop.co.uk

This company supply a wide range of organic fresh foods (meat, poultry, fruit and vegetables) and grocery items. They stock the range of Baby Organix, baby and weaning foods, many of which are gf/cf. They will deliver within 48 hours. You need to check their grocery items carefully for gluten and casein. They also stock a large variety of organic wines and spirits, in case you need fortifying! Their range is constantly expanding. Phone for a catalogue.

Orgran UK
PO Box 3577
London
NW2 1LQ
Tel: 020 8208 2966
Web: www.orgran.com

This company is based in Australia and was founded by two Italian brothers, so it should come as no surprise that they make a huge range of gf/cf pastas. Oh boy, do they make pasta. They make 27 varieties of pasta, all shapes, colours, sizes and flavours. As well as pasta they produce a variety of other gf/cf foods. Their goods are stocked in Tesco, Sainsbury's, Safeway, Morrison's, E. H. Booth, Holland and Barrett and almost every health food store in the country.

I recommend that you take a look at their website. It is very informative, with lots of recipes and one of the best (if not the best) nutritional information spreadsheets I've seen. They have even been kind enough to include a section on what in their range is safe for those who have candida.

All their range is also egg free and free from MSG and artificial flavourings, colourings and preservatives. Their gf/cf range includes:

- Pasta: 27 varieties are gf/cf and MSG free. All of these are egg free. There are 24 that are soya free. The pasta comes in all shapes, sizes, colours and flavours.
- Crispbreads – six varieties. All are egg and yeast free. All contain soya.
- Falafel mix – egg and yeast free. Contains soya.
- Vegetable minestrone mix – egg, yeast and soya free
- Egg replacer
- Buckwheat pancake mix
- Fat replacer – contains soya

- Apple and cinnamon pancake mix – contains soya
- Pizza and pastry multi-mix – contains soya
- Vegetarian bolognese – contains soya
- Corn cakes
- Fruit bars – contain soya
- Canned spaghetti
- Lite salsa corn cakes
- Lemon sponge pudding
- Chocolate sponge pudding

Parsonage Pork Ltd

The Parsonage
Llanboidy
Carmarthenshire
SA34 0HB
Tel/fax: 01994 448255

This company make a range of gf/cf sausages prepared to your own requirements. They also supply additive free ham and bacon. They will arrange delivery of your order.

Plamil Foods Ltd

Folkestone
Kent
CT19 6PQ
Tel: 01303 850588
Fax: 01303 850015

Plamil are a company that produce food for the vegan market, but by happy coincidence all their products are also gf/cf. All of their products are also free of genetically modified ingredients and free from artificial flavourings, colourings and preservatives. All their milks have added vitamins B2, B12, D2 and calcium.

Their products are available at a number of outlets, including health food stores. They do not sell to the general public, but I've included their contact details in case you require further information about their products. Their product range currently includes:

- ◦ Soya milk concentrate
- ◦ Soya milk, sugar free and ready to use
- ◦ Soya milk with apple juice
- ◦ White Sun – a milk substitute made from sunflower oil and pea protein
- ◦ White Sun with apple juice – as above
- ◦ Mayonnaise – egg free, in plain, garlic, tarragon or chilli flavours
- ◦ Chocolate – plain, mint, roasted hazelnut and 'Martello', a milk-less milk chocolate variety
- ◦ Organic chocolate – plain, orange, mint, 'Expressions', a milk-less milk chocolate variety, and chocolate drops
- ◦ Carob – plain, orange, roasted hazelnut, no-added sugar, and carob drops
- ◦ Carob spread

Provamel
Ashley House
86–94 High Street
Hounslow
Middlesex
TW3 1NH
Tel: 020 8577 2727
Fax: 020 8570 9364
Web: www.provamel.co.uk
Email: provamel@vdmuk-rs.co.uk

If your child has a soya intolerance, skip this entry, but otherwise read on, some prayers might be answered: in a word, ice-cream! This company has a huge range of soya-based products, most of which are gf/cf. Nearly all the supermarket chains stock at least some of the products and you would be hard pressed to find a health food shop that does not stock a lot of the range.

You will be pleased to know that it is Provamel's policy not to use genetically modified (GM) soya. They have a strict system of traceability and testing, to ensure that the soya they use is GM free. As a bonus, many of the products are enriched with calcium and some have riboflavin added.

Although it would be easier for me to list only those products that are not gf/cf, I will list those suitable, to let you know what to look out for.

- Junior yofu – yoghurts (available in peach, pear, strawberry and banana flavours; there are no lumpy fruit pieces in these)
- Yofu – yoghurts (available in natural, black cherry, vanilla, peach and mango, red cherry, peach and strawberry)
- Soya Dream – a single cream alternative
- Organic rice drink
- Ice desserts – ice cream (available in strawberry, chocolate and vanilla flavours)
- Soya alternative to milk – unsweetened, vanilla, chocolate, banana, strawberry, no added sugar or salt are all fine; beware, the plain sweetened variety contains gluten
- Soya desserts – beware, the version in pots is gf/cf, but the organic labelled dessert in cartons (available in vanilla and chocolate flavours) contains gluten

Pure Organics Ltd

Stockport Farm
Stockport Road
Amesbury
Wiltshire
SP4 7LN
Tel: 01980 626263
Fax: 01980 626264
Web: www.organics.org
Email: mail@organics.org

Pauline and Gary Stiles formed this company in 1996, after their eldest child was diagnosed as being autistic with severe learning difficulties. They set out to provide children's food that is organic and free from artificial additives. On top of this, all their product range (except chicken nuggets and pizzas) is gf/cf. None of their products contain nuts. At the time of going to press some of their range contained yeast extract. The company are reformulating all their range to exclude yeast extract which will eliminate all traces of MSG and make them suitable for Candida sufferers.

The products are available in all major supermarket chains, except Iceland. Tesco and Budgen's stock the entire range, the other stores carry only part of the range. Pure Organics say that if you have problems getting any of their products, phone them and they will find the closest store to you that stocks what you require. All the products are reasonably priced.

- Beefburgers
- Chicken burgers
- Pork sausages
- Beef mince
- Pork hulas
- Chicken hulas
- Beef hulas
- Lamb hulas

The product range is always being extended. It is well worth calling to get onto their mailing list, for further product news.

Schar

PO Box 126
Worcester
WR5 2ZN
Tel: 0808 1000 483 (freephone)
Web: www.schaer.com

This company produce a variety of foods that are gluten free. About half of their products are casein free too. The products that are suitable for the diet include:

- Margherita – a cake mix, contains maize
- Flour mix – contains maize
- Ertha – a premade sourdough bread, contains maize, apple juice and yeast
- Pane con soia vital – premade bread, contains maize, soya and yeast
- Baguette – part-cooked bread, contains maize and yeast
- Fantasia – ready-made sponge cake, contains egg and maize
- Brioches – ready-made cup cakes, contain egg and maize
- Magdalenas – ready-made sponge cakes, filled with apricot jam, contain egg and maize
- Savoiardi – ready-made sponge fingers, contain egg and maize
- Wafers al cacao – wafer biscuits with a chocolate filling, contain maize and soya

- Pasta – eight different varieties, all egg free, all contain maize; the lasagne also contains soya
- Fette biscottate – crispbread, contains soya, maize, egg and yeast
- Fette croccanti – cracker toast, contains maize
- Cialde wafer – waffle bread, contains maize and soya
- Pangrati – breadcrumbs, contains maize, soya, egg and yeast
- Musli – muesli, contains soya, maize, apple juice concentrate, raisins, dried apples and apricot

SHS International Ltd

100 Wavertree Boulevard
Wavertree International Technology Park
Liverpool
L7 9PT
Tel: 0151 228 8161
Email: info@shsint.co.uk

This company specialise in producing foods for a gluten free diet. Unfortunately, at present, only one of their product range is also casein free and is only available with a prescription: Harvest Mix.

Soya Health Foods Ltd

Unit 4 Guinness Road
Trafford Park
Manchester
M17 1SD
Tel: 0161 872 0549
Fax: 0161 872 6776

This company produce a range of cf food, but only their choc-ices are also gf. Sunrise carob ices are available in nearly all health food stores. There are six choc-ices to a pack. They are tasty and reasonably priced. The carob coating is not very thick, so even if your child doesn't usually like the taste of carob, you may find they enjoy these. As the company name suggests, they do contain soya.

Sunrise

See entry for **Soya Health Foods Ltd**.

Tofutti

Triano Brands Ltd
PO Box 1637
London
WC2E 9QQ
Tel: 020 8861 4443
Web: www.tofutti.co.uk

This company imports a range of cf foods, many of which are gf too. All products are soya based, but the soya is from a non GM source. Products include:

- ◦ 6 varieties of cream cheese (2 of which are organic)

- ◦ ice cream

Trufree

See entry for **Nutricia**.

Easy Reference Gf/ Cf Basic Foods Guide

This is to help you find the gf/cf basics you need easily. The addresses and telephone numbers for each supplier are listed in the Specialist Suppliers and Mail Order Directory. This section obviously duplicates a lot of the information that is contained there (although not as comprehensively), but it should help you locate what you need in a hurry and prevent you spending unnecessary time trawling through all the entries listed there. It should also give you a good idea of the variety available.

Much of the gf/cf food listed here is available from health food stores or by ordering through your local pharmacy. If you have trouble getting hold of the product you require, phone the manufacturer direct, and they will be able to tell you where your nearest outlet is.

Breads

- *Flax, corn and rice sourdough* (egg, soya and yeast free) by Sunnyvale.
  Available from Allergyfree Direct and Everfresh.

- *Mixed grain sourdough* (egg, soya and yeast free) by Sunnyvale.
  Available from Allergyfree Direct and Everfresh.

- *Sesame, corn and rice sourdough* (egg, soya and yeast free) by Sunnyvale.
  Available from Allergyfree Direct and Everfresh.

- *Sunflower seed, corn and rice sourdough* (egg, soya and yeast free) by Sunnyvale.
  Available from Allergyfree Direct and Everfresh.

- *Spicy onion bread* (egg, soya and yeast free) by Sunnyvale.
  Available from Allergyfree Direct and Everfresh.

- *Brown rice sliced bread* (available on prescription, egg and soya free, shelf-life 12 months) by Barkat.
  Also available from Allergyfree Direct and Gluten Free Foods.

- *White rice sliced bread* (available on prescription, egg and soya free) by Barkat.
  Also available from Allergyfree Direct and Gluten Free Foods.

- *Wholemeal sliced bread* (available on prescription, egg free) by Glutano.
  Also available from Allergyfree Direct and Gluten Free Foods.

- *Wholemeal par-baked bread* (available on prescription, egg free) by Glutano.
  Also available from Allergyfree Direct and Gluten Free Foods.

- *Rustic loaf* (par-baked baguette, available on prescription, egg, soya and corn free) by Pleniday.
  Also available from Brewhurst Health Food Supplies.

- *Sliced bread* (available on prescription, egg, soya and corn free) by Pleniday.
  Also available from Brewhurst.

- *Petit pain* (available on prescription, egg, soya and corn free) by Pleniday.
  Also available from Brewhurst.

- *Country loaf* (French cob style, available on prescription, egg, soya and corn free) by Pleniday.
  Also available from Brewhurst.

- *Bread mix* (egg and soya free) by Pleniday.
  Available from Brewhurst.

- *Brown rice bread* (available on prescription, egg, maize and soya free) by Ener-G.
  Also available from General Dietary.

- *Tapioca bread* (available on prescription, egg, maize and soya free) by Ener-G.
  Also available from General Dietary.

- *White rice bread* (available on prescription, egg, maize and soya free) by Ener-G.
  Also available from General Dietary.

- *Brown rice and maize bread* (available on prescription, egg and yeast free) by Ener-G.
  Also available from General Dietary.

- *Rice loaf* (available on prescription, egg, maize, soya and yeast free) by Ener-G.
  Also available from General Dietary.

- *Country french bread/pizza mix* (egg and soya free) by Gluten Free Pantry.
  Available from Gourmet Gluten-free Imports.

- *Tapioca bread mix* (egg, corn and soya free) by Gluten Free Pantry.
  Available from Gourmet Gluten-free Imports.

- *Ultra PKU, white sliced bread* (available on prescription, baked to order and delivered same day, suitable for freezing, egg, soya and maize free).
  Also available from Lifestyle Healthcare.

- *Ultra PKU, white unsliced bread* (as above).
  Also available from Lifestyle Healthcare.

- *Ultra PKU, brown sliced bread* (as above).
  Also available from Lifestyle Healthcare.

- *Ultra PKU, brown unsliced bread* (as above).
  Also available from Lifestyle Healthcare.

- *Ultra PKU, high fibre bread* (as above).
  Also available from Lifestyle Healthcare.

- *Ultra PKU, bread rolls* (as above, several varieties, white, brown, high fibre, bridge and onion).
  Available from Lifestyle Healthcare.

- *White bread mix* (available on prescription, soya, egg and corn free) by Dietary Specialities.
  Also available from Nutrition Point.

- *Brown bread mix* (as above) by Dietary Specialities.
  Also available from Nutrition Point.

- *Corn bread mix* (available on prescription, egg free) by Dietary Specialities.
  Also available from Nutrition Point.

- *White unsliced loaf.*
  Available from the Alternative Cake Company.

- *Brown unsliced loaf.*
  Available from the Alternative Cake Company.

- *Versaloaf* (add to water and the gf/cf flour of your choice to make a yeast free gf/cf bread).
  Available from Allergycare.

- *Eartha* (sourdough, contains maize and apple juice concentrate).
  Available from Schar.

- *Pane con soia vital* (ready-made bread, contains soya, maize and yeast).
  Available from Schar.

- *Baguette* (par-baked bread, contains maize and yeast).
  Available from Schar.

Biscuits and cookies

- *Apricot biscuits* (egg free) by Glutano.
  Available from Gluten Free Foods and Allergyfree Direct.

- *Ginger cookies* (egg free) by Glutano.
  Available from Gluten Free Foods and Allergyfree Direct.

- *Hazelnut cookies* (egg free) by Glutano.
  Available from Gluten Free Foods and Allergyfree Direct.

- *Chocolate cream filled wafers* (egg free) by Glutano.
  Available from Gluten Free Foods.

- *Lemon cookies* (egg and soya free) by Doves Farm.
  Available from Allergyfree Direct.

- *Organic chocolate rice cakes* (egg and corn free) by Kallo.
  Available from Allergyfree Direct.

- *Lemon biscuits* (soya and maize free) by Lifestyle.
  Available from Lifestyle Healthcare.

- *Orange and chocolate chip cookies* (as above) by Lifestyle.
  Available from Lifestyle Healthcare.

- *Peanut butter cookies* (as above) by Lifestyle.
  Available from Lifestyle Healthcare.

- *Ginger snaps* (as above) by Lifestyle.
  Available from Lifestyle Healthcare.

- *Chocolate chip cookies* (as above) by Lifestyle.
  Available from Lifestyle Healthcare.

- *Double chocolate chip cookies* (as above) by Lifestyle.
  Available from Lifestyle Healthcare.

- *Pecan and honey biscuits* (as above) by Lifestyle.
  Available from Lifestyle Healthcare.

- *Chocolate chip cookie mix* (egg and corn free) by Gluten Free Pantry.
  Available from Gourmet Gluten-free Imports.

- *Old fashioned cake and cookie mix* (egg, corn and soya free) by Gluten Free Pantry.
  Available from Gourmet Gluten-free Imports.

- *Sweet biscuits* (available on prescription, egg free) by Glutafin.
  Available from Nutricia Dietary Care.

- *Digestive biscuits* (available on prescription, egg free) by Glutafin.
  Available from Nutricia Dietary Care.

- *Tea biscuits* (available on prescription, egg free) by Glutafin.
  Available from Nutricia Dietary Care.

- *Bourbon biscuits* (egg free) by Glutafin.
  Available from Nutricia Dietary Care.

- *Custard creams* (egg free) by Glutafin.
  Available from Nutricia Dietary Care.

- *Chocolate chip cookies* (egg free) by Glutafin.
  Available from Nutricia Dietary Care.

- *Gingernut cookies* (egg free) by Glutafin.
  Available from Nutricia Dietary Care.

- *Shortcake biscuits* (egg free) by Glutafin.
  Available from Nutricia Dietary Care.

- *Ginger cookies* (egg, corn and soya free) by Pamela's.
  Available from Brewhurst.

- *Peanut butter cookies* (corn free) by Pamela's.
  Available from Brewhurst.

- *Savoiardi* – sponge fingers (contain egg and maize).
  Available from Schar.

- *Wafers al cacao* – chocolate-filled wafers (contain maize and soya).
  Available from Schar.

Cakes

- *White cake mix* (available on prescription, egg free) by Dietary Specialities.
  Also available from Nutrition Point.

- *Chocolate cake mix* (egg free) by Dietary Specialities.
  Available from Nutrition Point.

- *Bran muffin mix* (egg free) by Dietary Specialities.
  Available from Nutrition Point.

- *Banana bread mix* (egg free, contains dried banana) by Dietary Specialities.
  Available from Nutrition Point.

- *Brownie mix* (egg and soya free) by Dietary Specialities.
  Available from Nutrition Point.

- *Blueberry muffin mix* (egg free) by Dietary Specialities.
  Available from Nutrition Point.

- *Lemon muffins* (soya and maize free).
  Available from Lifestyle Healthcare.

- *Vanilla muffins* (soya and maize free).
  Available from Lifestyle Healthcare.

- *Old fashioned cake and cookie mix* (egg, corn and soya free) by
  Gluten Free Pantry.
  Available from Gourmet Gluten-free Imports.

- *Chocolate truffle brownies mix* (egg and soya free) by Gluten Free
  Pantry.
  Available from Gourmet Gluten-free Imports.

- *Muffins and quick bread mix* (egg and soya free) by Gluten Free
  Pantry.
  Available from Gourmet Gluten-free Imports.

- *Angel Food cake mix* (soya free) by Gluten Free Pantry.
  Available from Gourmet Gluten Free Imports.

- *Spice cake and gingerbread mix* (egg, soya and corn free) by Gluten
  Free Pantry.
  Available from Gourmet Gluten-free Imports.

- *Banana cake* by Glutafin.
  Available from Nutricia Dietary Care.

- *Lemon madeira cake* by Glutafin.
  Available from Nutricia Dietary Care.

- *Date and walnut cake* by Glutafin.
  Available from Nutricia Dietary Care.

- *Coconut cakes* by Pleniday.
  Available from Brewhurst.

- *Raisin and fruit cake* by Pleniday.
  Available from Brewhurst.

- *Madeleine cakes* by Pleniday.
  Available from Brewhurst.

- *Raisin madeleines* by Pleniday.
  Available from Brewhurst.

- *Cake mix* (egg and soya free) by Pleniday.
  Available from Brewhurst.

- *Fantasia* – sponge cake mix (contains egg and maize).
  Available from Schar.

- *Brioches* – ready-made sponge cup cakes (contain egg and maize).
  Available from Schar.

- *Magdelenas* – cup cakes filled with apricot jam (contain egg and maize).
  Available from Schar.

- *Celebration cake* – plain or iced.
  Available from Alternative Cake Company.

- *Just Fruit cake.*
  Available from Alternative Cake Company.

- *Made to order cakes.*
  The Alternative Cake Company are happy to make a variety of cakes for special occasions that are gf/cf. Contact for details.

Flours

Many health food shops stock a wide range of gf flours. It may take some trial and error to find a good quality flour that you are happy with. Remember, when ordering, to check the weights of the goods on offer, as they can vary greatly from supplier to supplier and this will affect the value for money aspect.

Never buy gf flours from a shop where they operate a help-yourself, scoop what you want from a storage container system. The risk of cross-contamination from gluten-containing flours is far too great.

If you are intending to follow any of the recipes in this book, it is worth noting that 99 per cent of them are made from a combination of white rice flour, tapioca starch and potato starch. Don't forget to order some xanthan gum; you will notice the difference.

- *White rice flour* – available from Barbara's Kitchen and Innovative Solutions.

- *Brown rice flour* – available from Allergycare (organic), Doves Farm and Innovative Solutions.

- *Buckwheat flour* – available from Allergycare (organic) and Doves Farm.

- *Tapioca starch flour* – available from Allergycare (organic), Barbara's Kitchen, Gourmet Gluten-free Imports and Innovative Solutions.

- *Sago flour* – available from Allergycare (organic).

- *Millet flour* – available from Allergycare (organic).

- *Potato starch flour* – available from Barbara's Kitchen, Gourmet Gluten-free Imports and Innovative Solutions.

- *Gluten free flours* – available from Doves Farm (an all-purpose flour, containing rice, potato, buckwheat and maize flours); Innovative Solutions (all-purpose flour containing white and brown rice flour, potato flour and tapioca flour); Nutrition Point (plain flour substitute, soya free); and Schar (all-purpose flour, contains maize).

- *Maize flour* – available from Doves Farm.

- *Gram flour* – available from Doves Farm.

- *Fibre mix* – available from Nutricia Health Care and Nutrition Point.

- *Multigrain flour* – available from Nutricia Health Care.

- *Multigrain fibre* – available from Nutricia Health Care.

- *Xanthan gum* (not a flour, but vital for gf baking) – available from Barbara's Kitchen and Innovative Solutions.

- *Guar gum* (can be used as a substitute for xanthan gum) – available from Gourmet Gluten-free Imports.

Pasta

There is a huge range of gf/cf pastas. You can get a variety of shapes, sizes, colours and flavoured pasta. I have found gf/cf pasta to vary widely in both quality and cost. Unfortunately, the cost is no indication of quality. Whether you go for a soya-, corn- or rice-based pasta is up to you, but if your child has an aversion to strong smells and tastes, then you may be better off trying rice-based pasta first.

Many supermarkets are now stocking some ranges of gf/cf pastas and you will be spoilt for choice in your health food shop.

The list for pastas is very long, as each company makes several different varieties, shapes, colours, etc. In an effort not to destroy any more of the rain forest than is necessary and because they are so easily available, I will not list them all separately.

If your child has never tried/liked pasta before, you can always try rice noodles. Sharwood's make a very nice rice noodle that is gf/cf and it is stocked in every supermarket I have ever been in. It is also considerably cheaper than gf/cf pastas.

Milks

The variety here is quite dazzling. The majority of supermarkets do their own ranges of gf/cf soya milks, plain, sweetened and flavoured, that are very reasonably priced. Some of these supermarket brands are also organic in origin. Be careful when buying sweetened or flavoured soya milks, as these can have a trace of gluten in them.

Be warned that at the time of going to press, Rice Dream, a rice-based milk substitute, is not suitable for inclusion on this diet as the rice is processed in such a way that a barley wash is used. This leaves behind very tiny traces of gluten. There is some debate as to whether this trace of barley will cause any damage to our children and until this has been settled, it is best to err on the side of caution and avoid the product.

Apart from these supermarket brands, the following are also gf/cf:

- *Soya milk powder* by Allergycare.
  Available direct from the company or at selected health food stores.

- *Rice milk powder* by Allergycare (as above).

- *Milkshake powder* by Allergycare, soya based (as above).

- *Soya milk concentrate* by Plamil, with added B2, B12, D2 and calcium.
  Available at health food stores.

- *Soya milk, sugar free* by Plamil (as above).

- *White sun* by Plamil (a milk substitute made from sunflower oil and pea protein).
  Available from health food stores.

- *Soya alternative to milk* by Provamel, in unsweetened, vanilla, chocolate, banana and strawberry flavours (warning: their plain organic sweetened variety contains gluten).
  Available in health food stores and some supermarkets.

- *Soya Dream* by Provamel (a single cream alternative).
  Available from health food stores.

- *Rice alternative to milk* by Provamel.
  Available from health food stores.

Desserts

There are quite a few desserts available that are gf/cf. Among those that are easiest to find in supermarkets and health food stores are:

- *Imagine puddings* by Imagine (rice syrup-based and available in a range of flavours – vanilla, chocolate, butterscotch, banana and lemon).
  Available from Clearspring and health food stores.

- *Junior yofu* by Provamel (yoghurts available in peach and pear flavour and strawberry and banana flavour (no fruit lumps).
  Available from health food stores and selected supermarkets.

- *Yofu* by Provamel (yoghurts available in natural, black cherry, vanilla, peach and mango, red cherry, peach and strawberry flavours).
  Available from health food stores and selected supermarkets.

○ *Ice desserts* by Provamel (soya-based ice cream, available in strawberry, vanilla and chocolate flavours).
Available from health food stores.

○ *Soya deserts* by Provamel (soya-based desserts (not yoghurts), available in vanilla and chocolate flavours); only buy the version in four pots that are joined together as the organic version in a large carton contains gluten.
Available in health food stores.

○ *Choc-ices* by Sunrise/Soya Health Foods (soya-based ice cream, coated in carob).
Available from health food stores.

○ *Sponge puddings* by Organ (lemon and chocolate flavours, soya free).
Available from health food stores.

The Advanced Diet

I have deliberately put this section towards the back of the book, so as not to scare the living daylights out of you. Just when you thought you'd covered all the basics and done everything that you need to do diet-wise, I spring this on you. Sorry.

I don't know if you will find this any consolation, but you will have done the hardest bit already by removing gluten, casein, MSG and aspartame from the diet. The pyramid below gives a very straightforward and graphic representation of the way to progress with treating your child via their diet.

The removal of gluten and casein from your child's diet, the first level of the pyramid, has already been covered and you will doubtlessly be grateful that I will not go through it all again.

The second level of the pyramid is the removal of all synthetic E numbers. The important bit here is the word synthetic. E numbers are just a type of shorthand, a quick way of expressing what can be very long and complex names. The vast majority of the E numbers are safe to include in your child's diet and have no side effects at all, so please do not reject all foods that include E numbers without finding out more on the subject.

To be able to do the subject of E numbers justice, I really would have to write another book. But there is no need to fear that I will be doing this, as there already is an excellent book on the market which covers the subject in more depth than I could ever hope to achieve. I strongly recommend that you purchase a copy of Maurice Hanssen's book *E for Additives* (more details in the Further Reading section). Please do not rely on the various lists regarding E numbers that do the rounds (via the Internet, fax or post), as I have found many of them to be highly inaccurate in their information. If Hanssen's book leaves you feeling that you don't know where to begin removing the E numbers from your child's diet, I would suggest that you

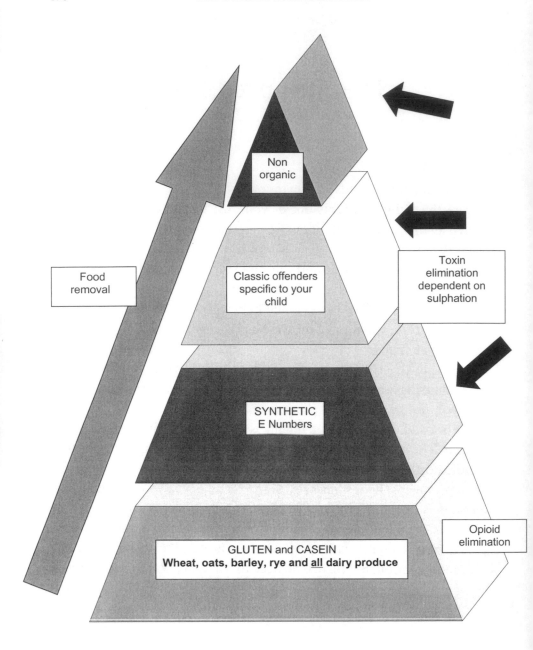

Reproduced with the kind permission of AiA

could do worse than begin with Hanssen's list of E numbers in the chapter 'The avoidable 57 additives'.

The third level of the pyramid deals with foods that are specific to your child. Again, the important bit to remember here is that you should only be concerned with the foods that *your* child is unable to tolerate, not anyone else's child. Although many of the children on this diet seem unable to tolerate similar foods, this is usually, but not wholly, due to how well the child's sulphation system is working. If this is starting to sound confusing, then I would recommend you read some of the scientific papers regarding the sulphation process in autistic children, which appear in the Further Reading section of the book.

The foods that your child is most likely to have an intolerance to are: apples, all citrus fruits, bananas, melons, raspberries, grapes and tomatoes. The fruits that are most tolerated by children on this diet are: pineapple, pear, peaches, apricots and strawberries in moderation.

It is likely that your child will have allergies all of their very own. I will not bore you with a list of Jack's other allergies, as they will not have any relevance to your child. These are quite easy for me to cope with when cooking for Jack, especially when compared to removing gluten and casein.

So how will you know which foods are causing problems for your child? Trust me, you will know. After your child has been free from gluten and casein for a while, you will notice that sometimes your child will not be their usual self (their 'new gf/cf self'). Once you have double checked that gluten and/or casein have not managed to sneak into your child's diet, you will feel at a loss to know what is the cause. This is why it is so important to keep a food diary for your child, even many months into the gf/cf diet. You will, with the aid of this diary, soon be able to pinpoint the food that your child eats that coincides with their 'slipping back'. By elim-inating the suspect food from your child's diet, you will be able to see if there is an improvement to their behaviour, sleep, etc. or not. If you think you have got the right food source, you can always double check by letting your child have a very small amount of the suspect food and seeing if their behaviour slips back again.

But please remember, that not every time your child is behaving differ-ently will it be down to a bad reaction to food. Like everyone else, our children will 'get out of their beds the wrong side' and be in a bad mood for no apparent reason. Sometimes, they might be in the early stages of an illness. Other times, it can just be that there has been a dramatic routine change or something else that you cannot fathom, which has caused them to 'not be themselves'.

Of course, sometimes the reaction can be so extreme that you are left in absolutely no doubt that it is a food that is causing the problem and which particular food it is. One lunchtime Jack drank a small tumbler of a particular brand of blackcurrant drink, for the first (and only) time; three hours later he was so hyperactive that he was bouncing off the walls. I had never (even in the pre-diet days) seen him in such a state. When he was still awake five hours after his normal bedtime, I was getting in quite a state too.

Sometimes it can be far harder to track down the source of the problem. I had noticed that whenever Jack got ill, he would completely lose bladder and bowel control for one to two weeks. I couldn't work out how various different illnesses could all make him doubly incontinent. Then the penny dropped: the only thing that all his illnesses had in common was the way I treated them. At the first sign of illness, I would give him a dose of a child's paracetamol suspension liquid and keep giving it to him, until he got better. The next time he was ill, I silently apologised to Jack, and did not give him any medication at all. This time he retained bowel and bladder control. I only mention this as many of the children on the diet have a problem with paracetamol suspension and other medications that contain paracetamol. The reactions are too various to list. If this appears to be a problem for your child, contact your GP about other pain-relief to use. It should go without saying that if your child is running a high temperature contact your GP or take your child straight to AE.

Other times you will have the feeling that you haven't quite got there yet with your child. I often saw glimpses of a different (better) Jack, but he'd never stay very long. I was stumped. Then I took aspartame out of Jack's diet. I have already admitted to doing this very late. I had no idea of its effects. When I found out, I removed it immediately. It took a while for me to see any results (a couple of weeks, rather than a few days), but I did, finally, get the Jack of whom I had so many tantalising glimpses.

So the rule of finding out if there are any foods that cause a reaction specific to your child is to keep a very detailed food and drink diary. I know that it can be a bore and time consuming, but it really pays dividends at the end of the day.

The final part of the pyramid is the elimination of non-organic food. Ideally we should all be eating organic food. At the moment it can be difficult and costly, although organic food is getting cheaper and more widely available. But sadly for those children who are most seriously affected, they will react badly to the pesticides and other chemicals present in non-organic foods. Because of this, they will need to eat only organic foods. Regardless of the severity of your child's condition, please try to incorporate as much organic food into their diet as possible.

Candida

By now you will have noticed that I have mentioned (just a few times!) that Jack has candida. You may well have noticed from the recipes and Specialist Suppliers Directory that I have warned if foods contain yeast or yeast extract, or if they are not suitable if your child has candida. The reason that I have done this is not just because Jack suffers from candida, but because a significant number of children on the diet also have candida. There may well be even more children who suffer from this, but as yet they have not been diagnosed.

In the most basic terms, candida is a thrush-like infection of the gut. That's it. There are many, many books and also information on the Internet about candida, if you want to know more. To discuss it fully here would take far too long. Talking from personal experience (the only sort I am qualified to talk from), the difference that diagnosis and treatment for candida made to Jack was startling. Not as startling as the diet has been, I will be the first to admit, but startling never the less. Conventional treatment for candida is very simple – sugar free Nystatin, taken orally and diet modification. You can easily check if your child has candida: it is merely a case of asking your GP to have a stool sample from your child tested. A note of caution: some of the children on the diet who do have candida get back a negative result. If you have read about candida and are convinced that your child suffers from this, but you get back a negative result, I would strongly suggest that you contact AiA for advice.

Directory of Useful Contacts

Allergy induced Autism (AiA)
Membership Secretary
8 Hollie Lucas Road
Kings Heath
Birmingham
B13 0QL
Tel: 01733 331771
Web: *Allergy-induced-Autism.co.uk* or *AutismMedical.com* or *autismdiet.co.uk*

Please consider joining AiA, if you have not already done so. As well as an information pack, resource book and a quarterly newsletter, you will be accessing a mine of information and be kept abreast of the latest research, developments and changes. It is also a good way of finding others in your area who are following the diet to swap tips and act as an informal support network. I, for one, could not have managed to implement the diet as successfully as I did without the support and knowledge of AiA. Also, for the pittance of the annual membership fee, I have worked out that in the first year alone I saved nearly six times that amount in free and reduced price offers from suppliers of gf/cf foods.

Autism Research Unit
School of Health Sciences
University of Sunderland
Sunderland
SR2 7EE
Tel: 0191 510 8922
Fax: 0191 567 0420
Web: www.osiris.sunderland.ac.uk/aut-cgi/homepage
Email: aru@sunderland.ac.uk

Home of the famous Sunderland Test. This is one of only three centres in the world (and the only one in the UK) where you can have your child tested for the casein and gluten peptides. This is the place to go to get the piece of paper to prove (or disprove) that your child will benefit from the gf/cf diet. Contact for information about the test and how to have your child tested. The phone lines are almost constantly engaged (I did say it was famous), so it may be quicker to fax or email.

The Coeliac Society

PO Box 220
High Wycombe
Buckinghamshire
HP11 2HY
Tel: 01494 437278
Fax: 01494 474349
Email: memsec@coeliac.co.uk
Web: www.coeliac.co.uk

It is only very recently that parents of autistic children on the gf/cf diet have been able to join the Coeliac Society. The membership is free, although a donation is appreciated. You get sent a pocket book listing all the gluten free foods from major manufacturers, a list of prescribable foods and access to updates, etc. All this is very welcome, but please remember that the information sent to you covers only part of the diet (it does not cover casein, MSG and aspartame), and that our children tend to be sensitive to foods that most coeliacs can tolerate, e.g. malt flavouring.

It is worth joining, as the food listing alone will save you a fortune in phone calls to food manufacturers to check the source of starch, food starch, edible starch, modified starch, etc., as the list contains only foods with a gf starch source.

National Autistic Society

393 City Road
London
EC1V 1NG
Tel: 020 7833 2299
Fax: 020 7833 9666
Web: www.oneworld.org/autism_uk/nas@nas.org.uk

Major supermarket chains

Phone and ask for the customer services department and ask for lists of their gluten and milk free products to be sent to you. Word of warning: do not ask for a casein free list – it tends to confuse them. Unfortunately, only a few supermarket chains currently provide an MSG list. But ask anyway; one day, if enough people ask, they might produce one. Then, when the two lists arrive, you need to cross-reference them. Don't worry, it's not as daunting as it sounds – it only takes about half an hour, at the most. All the supermarkets I have contacted have been happy to find out the ingredients and their sources, when I have phoned to enquire about a specific product.

You do need to remain vigilant. Not only will you need to check for MSG in each product when you shop, but it is also worth checking the ingredients each time you buy, in case the company have reformulated the product. One supermarket that will remain nameless added barley to a children's breakfast cereal that Jack had been happy to eat. They added barley to the ingredients list, but neglected to remove the gluten free label from the side of the packet!

Asda
Tel: 0500 100 055 (freephone)
Web: www.asda.co.uk

Boots
Tel: 0845 070 8090

CWS/Co-op
Tel: 0800 317 827 (freephone)
Web: www.co-op.co.uk

Gateway/Kwik Save/Somerfield
Tel: 020 8935 9359
Web: www.somerfield.co.uk

Iceland
Tel: 01244 842 842
Web: www.Iceland.co.uk

Marks and Spencer

Tel: 020 7268 1234

Web: www.marks-and-spencer.co.uk

Morrison's

Tel: 01924 870 000

Sainsbury

Tel: 0800 636 262 (freephone)

Web: www.sainsburys.co.uk

Tesco

Tel: 0800 505 555 (freephone)

Web: www.tesco.co.uk

Waitrose

Tel: 01344 424 975

Web: www.waitrose.co.uk

It is worth pointing out, that at the time this book went to press, Iceland have been good enough to produce just one booklet to cover all of their own-label foods. It covers those products that are vegetarian and free of gluten/milk/soya/egg. There is no need to cross reference, as it has all been done for you. They also guarantee that the whole range of their own-brand foods are free from GM foods, artificial colours and flavours and MSG, although they do use HVP and yeast extract, which naturally contain traces of MSG. This, combined with their extensive range of organic foods at 'normal' prices, means that if you are not lucky enough to have an Iceland store near you, you should start campaigning to get one! Let's hope all the other supermarkets take note and follow their lead.

Major UK food manufacturers

Best Foods UK Ltd

Tel: 0800 435 562 (freephone)

Product lines include the brands:

- Knorr
- Mazola
- Bovril
- Marmite
- Napolina
- Hellmann's
- Brown & Polson.

Birds Eye

Consumer Care Dept
Station Avenue
Walton-on-Thames
Surrey
KT12 1NT
Tel: 0800 332 277 (freephone)

Britvic Soft Drinks Ltd

Britvic House
Broomfield Road
Chelmsford
Essex
CM1 1TU
Tel: 01245 261871

Range includes:

- Bass
- Britvic
- Corona
- Idris
- Juice up
- Quosh
- R. Whites
- Robinsons
- Tango
- Top Deck.

Cadburys

Tel: 0121 451 4444 (see also notes for Trebor)

As you might expect, none of Cadbury's confectionery is suitable for inclusion on the diet. Although they do a small range of chocolate that does not contain milk, it does contain a small amount of butterfat that contains traces of lactose. It isn't all doom and gloom here, as their cocoa powder is gf/cf and is great for cooking with.

Centura Foods

Booth Lane
Middlewich
Cheshire
CW10 0HD
Tel: 01606 834747

Range includes:

- Bisto
- Frank Coopers
- Paxo
- Robertsons
- Saxa

Coca Cola Schweppes Ltd

Charter Place
Vine Street
Uxbridge
Middlesex
UB8 1ST
Tel: 0800 227 711 (freephone)

Range includes:

- Canada Dry
- Cresta
- Coca-Cola
- Dr Pepper
- Gina

- ○ Kia-Ora
- ○ Oasis
- ○ Roses
- ○ Schweppes
- ○ Sunkist

Colmans
Tel: 0800 281 026 (freephone)

Most famous for their mustards but also provide a huge range of packet and ready-made sauces.

Del Monte
Tel: 01784 447 400

This company do not produce a list of gf/cf foods, because all their food and drink range is free from gluten. With the exception of their Frutini in creamy sauce range, all their products are also free from milk derivatives. In addition to this, their products are also free from: nuts, sesame derivatives, egg derivatives, wheat and maize derivatives, glutamates (hurrah!), benzoates, sulphites, soya derivatives and artificial colour (except fruit cocktail and Frutini strawberry jelly).

I've included their telephone number, as it is worth periodically checking with them that they haven't changed their policy.

Heinz
Tel: 020 8573 7757
Web: www.heinz.co.uk

This company has an amazing website that lists the ingredients for every one of their products. The site is updated on a regular basis.

HP Foods Ltd
Tower Road
Aston Cross
Birmingham
B6 5AB
Tel: 0121 359 4911

Brands include:

- Amoy
- Daddies
- HP
- Lea & Perrins.
- Rajah

Homepride
Web: www.homepride.co.uk

Brands include:

- Campbell's
- Fray Bentos
- Homepride.

Kellogg's
Tel: 0800 626 066 (freephone)

Warning: all the Kellogg's products that are listed as gf contain traces of hordein (barley protein), in the malt flavouring that is used. It is termed gluten free because the Coeliac Society (UK) has included it in its list of foods suitable for inclusion in a gf diet. However, many parents with children on the diet have said that their children react to foods containing malt flavouring and this is probably best to avoid.

Kerry Foods
Tel: 01784 430 777

Brand names include:

- Walls
- Richmond
- Mattessons.

KP Foods UK
PO Box 4
Ashby-Dela-Zouch
Leicestershire

LE65 2UQ
Tel: 01530 412 771

Produce a wide variety of crisps, peanuts and other snacks. Their gf and cf lists are very extensive but unfortunately most of these contain MSG.

McCain Foods (GB) Ltd
Tel: 01723 584141

McCormick
Tel: 01844 292930

Manufacture a huge range of herbs, spices and seasonings under the name of Schwartz. Many of their products are gf/cf and they've even managed to produce all the information within one brochure, so there is no need to cross-reference two booklets.

Mars UK
Tel: 01753 550 055 (ask for external relations department)

There are no Mars chocolate products that are suitable, but some of their confectionery range is, e.g. Starburst (to anyone over the age of 20 years, you will know them better as Opal Fruits).

Matthews Foods Plc
Tel: 01924 272 534

Manufacture the Pure range of margarines. There are several different varieties. I have found the Pure sunflower margarine great for cooking, baking and spreading. It is available in nearly all supermarkets and health food shops.

Nestlé
Tel: 01904 604604

Although Nestlé are best known as makers of confectionery, they also manufacture some well-known food brands, i.e.:

- Libby's

- Crosse & Blackwell
- Rowntrees
- Creations
- Gales
- Sunpat
- Sarsons
- Buitoni.

You may be pleased to know that they do a range of sweets that are gf/cf and MSG free and readily available in newsagents.

Pedigree Masterfoods
Tel: 0800 952 1234

Produce products under the brands:

- Dolmio
- Uncle Ben's
- Tyne Brand.

Premier Brands UK Ltd
Tel: 0845 602 2020

Their product range is mainly beverages, including cocoa powder (useful for cooking with).

J. A. Sharwood & Co. Ltd
Tel: 01784 473 000

Produce an extensive list of Chinese and Indian foods, sauces and ingredients that are gf/cf.

After a quick look at their products in my local supermarket I was surprised to find that many of them are MSG free too, but as they do not produce a list to cover this, you will need to check each individual product yourself, when you plan to purchase it.

Supercook
Tel: 01977 684937

Produce a wide range of baking goods and aids. Unfortunately they do not at the moment produce lists of gf/cf products. They will, however, check individual products for you and do so very thoroughly.

Trebor Bassett
Tel: 0121 451 4432

Cadbury owns Trebor. Make sure when you phone that you ask for the Trebor Bassett product list. If you don't, you will get a letter telling you that all of Cadbury's products contain milk.

If you thought your child would never be able to eat sweets again, then this should be a very pleasant surprise. The list of gf/cf sweets is huge. Your biggest problem will be trying to memorise them!

Trebor do point out that the glucose syrups which are used in the manufacture of their sweets are made from either wheat or maize and these are used interchangeably. The intense heat treatment used when processing glucose syrup means that all proteins are destroyed. As gluten is a protein, this too will be destroyed and is therefore considered suitable for inclusion in the gf/cf diet.

Unilever
Tel: 020 7822 5252
Web: www.unilever.com

Brands include:

- Batchelors
- Findus
- Oxo
- Ragu.

Brand-name foods – quick reference
If you need to check the source of an ingredient in a product, but don't know who owns the brand, see the list below.

- Amoy – HP
- Batchelors – Unilever
- Bisto – Centura Foods

- Bovril – Best Foods
- Brown & Polson – Best Foods
- Buitoni – Nestlé
- Campbell's – Homepride
- Creations – Nestlé
- Crosse & Blackwell – Nestlé
- Daddies – HP
- Dolmio – Pedigree Masterfoods
- Findus – Unilever
- Frank Coopers – Centura Foods
- Fray Bentos – Homepride
- Gales – Nestlé
- Hellmann's – Best Foods
- Homepride – Homepride
- HP – HP
- Knorr – Best Foods
- Lea & Perrins – HP
- Libby's – Nestlé
- Marmite – Best Foods
- Mattessons – Kerry Foods
- Mazola – Best Foods
- Napolina –Best Foods
- Oxo – Unilever
- Paxo – Centura Foods
- Ragu – Unilever
- Rajah – HP Foods
- Richmond – Kerry Foods
- Robertsons – Centura Foods
- Rowntrees – Nestlé
- Sarsons – Nestlé
- Saxa – Centura Foods
- Schwartz – McCormick
- Sunpat – Nestlé
- Trebor – Cadbury
- Trebor Bassett – Cadbury
- Tyne Brand – Pedigree Masterfoods
- Uncle Ben's – Pedigree Masterfoods
- Walls – Kerry Foods

Fast food chains

Burger King
Tel: 01895 206000
Web: www.burgerking.co.uk

Very good website, with in-depth information on ingredients of their foods and suitability for various allergies.

McDonald's
Tel: 020 8700 7000
Web: www.McDonald's.co.uk

Suppliers of nutritional supplements

I have listed a few companies who supply vitamin and mineral supplements, as many of the products that are sold commercially in supermarkets and chemists can contain gluten and/or casein and it can be difficult to tell. As always, please check with the individual suppliers that the products you intend to use are gf/cf.

Biocare Ltd
Tel: 0121 433 3727

Bioscience Ltd
Tel: 01892 543 502

Nutrition Associates
Tel: 01904 691 591

Quest Vitamins
Tel: 0121 359 0056

Miscellaneous

The Soil Association
Tel: 0117 929 0661

This organisation produces a directory of places where you can purchase all manner of organic goods, all over the UK.

GFCFkidsuk@egroups.com

A UK based support group for parents following the gf/cf diet. A mine of information, support and advice.

www.gfcfdiet.com

This is an American website compiled by parents and professionals. It is a great source of information, recipes, ideas and technical information, etc.

www.AutismNDI@aol.com

The site for ANDI – the American Network for Dietary Intervention. ANDI is AiA's sister organisation in America. Great website, lots of information on gf/cf diet and loads of recipes.

GFCFrecipes@egroups.com

An American based group providing gf/cf recipes.

www.autism.com/ari

The website for the Autism Research Unit, in San Diego. The unit is the 'home' of the famous Bernard Rimmler and it provides a wealth of information about autism, the latest research and treatments. It is also the organiser of the annual DAN (Defeat Autism Now) conferences.

Hyperactive Children's Support Group
Tel: 01903 725182 (Mon–Fri 10 am–3 pm)
c/o Sally Bunday
71 Whyke Lane
Chichester
West Sussex
PO19 2LD

For information send an SAE, 9 x 4 inches.

www.gfmall.com

This is a website devoted to companies who produce and/or sell gluten free food. A lot of the food is also casein free. Many of the companies are based outside the UK, but it will inform you where you can get their products here. Worth viewing to get an idea of what is available, and it is updated regularly, with more companies adding their details.

www.gluten-free.org/reichelt.html

This site has 27 abbreviated articles by Kalle Reichelt MD, a pioneer in the study and research of autism and diets.

www.autismuk.com

This is the website for the Society for the Autistically Handicapped. It is a huge and well-thought out website, which deals with many aspects of autism and the treatments and therapies. It is a mine of information and research and also has many relevant and interesting link sites.

www.oneworld.org/autism-uk

This is the National Autistic Society's website. It has various web links and general information on autism and the work of the Society. It also has a very good question and answer page about the diet with Paul Shattock of the Autism Research Unit.

www.NoMilk.com

A huge site with many, many useful links to other dairy free sites. Covers general information on a dairy free diet, scientific/medical research, specialist suppliers, recipes and loads more.

Glossary

This section, I hope, will help to inform you as you start to enter the weird and wonderful world of food labelling.

I got fed up (and still do), with people looking at the list of Jack's forbidden foods and asking 'What's that?' and pointing to some obscure ingredient that I had yet to find in any food. I'd mumble, 'It contains gluten', and silently pray that they didn't follow it up with, 'Yes, but what is it?'

In the beginning, I stuck religiously to the list of forbidden food ingredients, whenever I went shopping. Then, as the diet progressed and I saw the effect that it had on Jack, I started to get curious (for that, read paranoid), about all the other ingredients appearing on the labels of the food I was buying that I didn't have a clue about. Could they affect him? Were they all right? If I didn't know what something was, did I want him to eat it? Was I rejecting perfectly good food, through ignorance?

This is not a list of forbidden or acceptable foods. It is my hope that this glossary will inform you, enable you to make informed decisions about the foods you purchase, allow you to speak with knowledge about the diet to others and prevent you falling into some of the traps that I did.

Acacia gum – gf/cf. Derived from a plant and used as a thickener, emulsifier, stabiliser and gelling agent.

Agar (Agar-agar) – gf/cf. A tasteless white powder made from seaweed. It is used by the food industry as a thickening agent, owing to its gelling properties. It is commonly used as a vegetarian substitute for gelatine.

Anti-caking agents – added to foods (usually powders), to prevent them clumping together, by allowing them to flow freely. Magnesium carbonate is commonly used, but they can be from a gluten source, so check if not stated on the label.

Arrowroot – gf/cf. Used as a thickening agent.

Bicarbonate of soda – gf/cf.

Buckwheat – gf/cf. Despite its name, it does not contain wheat. It is a member of the rhubarb family. Only the seed is used and it is either ground into flour or flakes. It has a nutty taste.

Buckwheat groats – gf/cf. Crushed and hulled buckwheat.

Bulgar – a wheat product. Contains gluten.

Caramel colouring – it is best to check any products containing this, as more often than not it will contain lactose and barley malt syrup.

Carob bean gum – gf/cf. See **locust bean gum**.

Carrageenan – gf/cf. Extracted from seaweed. Used in the food industry as a stabiliser, thickener and gelling agent.

Cassava – see **tapioca**.

Cocoa butter – gf/cf. Despite its name, it does not contain butter. It is simply the oil of the cocoa plant.

Cornstarch – gf/cf. The American term for cornflour.

Corn syrup – compound of fructose (fruit sugar) and dextrose (corn sugar), commonly used in food production. Although it is gf/cf, many people in the general population are allergic to it. Watch for any reaction in your child before deciding to remove it from their diet.

Couscous – semolina, which has been processed into small pellets. Contains gluten.

Cream of tartar – gf/cf.

Dextrin – an incomplete hydrolysed starch. The starch can have many origins – corn, maize, potato, wheat, rice, and tapioca. As you can see, most of the starches that can be used are gf, but you will need to check each product with the manufacturer.

Dextrose – gf/cf. This is the sugar derived from corn.

Diglycerides – in the UK, these usually originate from corn. Wheat is occasionally used. In the USA, wheat is more commonly used than corn. You will need to check with the manufacturer.

Emulsifiers – gf/cf. These are added to a food product to prevent any liquid and fat or oil from separating. Most commonly derived from plants. Guar gum, xanthan gum and lecithin are the most commonly used emulsifiers.

Flax – gf/cf. This is not commonly used in food production, but is a good source of dietary fibre.

Farina – gf/cf. In the UK this is the name for potato starch flour.

Fu – dried wheat gluten.

Gari – see **tapioca**.

Gelatine – gf/cf.

Glucono delta lactone – gf/cf. Anti-caking agent. This is a type of sugar derived from grapes. Despite its name it contains neither gluten nor lactose. Commonly used in baking when yeast is not being used.

Glucose syrup – Produced from a variety of food starches, most commonly corn or wheat. The heat treatment process ensures all protein (including gluten) is destroyed.

Gram flour – gf/cf. The flour made from lentils.

Guar gum – gf/cf. This is used frequently in gf products to 'replace' gluten and by the food industry as a whole, as a thickener or emulsifier. Made from guar seeds. It is rich in fibre, but it can have a mild laxative effect if consumed in excess.

Gum arabic – gf/cf. Another term for acacia gum.

Hordein – This is the barley protein that is commonly found in malt flavourings. The Coeliac Society permits this. Many parents on the diet have noticed bad reactions when their child has consumed a food containing it.

Hydrolysed protein – It can originate from all sorts of things, including gluten, casein and yeast. This will nearly always contain traces of naturally occurring (from its manufacturing process) MSG.

Hydrolysed vegetable protein – as above.

HVP – as above.

Japanese isinglass – gf/cf. Another term for agar.

Job's tears – American term for pearl barley. Contains gluten.

Kamut – high protein version of wheat. Contains gluten.

Kasha – gf/cf. This is another name for buckwheat.

Lecithin – gf/cf. This is used as an emulsifier. It is most commonly derived from soya. It is less commonly derived from egg yolk, peanuts or maize.

Liquorice – derived from liquorice root, which is gf, but it is mixed with wheat flour during processing and so all sweets containing liquorice contain gluten. This includes solid liquorice sweets and liquorice ropes.

Liquorice flavouring – gf/cf. This is primarily used in the manufacture of boiled sweets.

Locust bean gum – gf/cf. This gum is derived from the locust/carob tree. It is rich in protein. It has many uses in the food industry, as a thickener, emulsifier, binder, gelling agent and stabiliser.

Malic acid – gf/cf. This can be derived from apples or pears. It is now most commonly chemically derived. It is worth checking if you are eliminating apples from your child's diet.

Malt – produced by steeping barley in water and allowing it to germinate or sprout. Contains gluten.

Malt extract/malt extract flavouring – these are both prepared from barley and are used in small amounts as flavour enhancers. They have been shown to contain a small amount of the barley protein, hordein.

Maltodextrin – despite the malt prefix, in the UK this is generally made from corn and will be gf. If in doubt contact the manufacturer.

Manioc – see **tapioca**.

Millet – gf/cf. This cereal has a high protein and low starch content. It contains all of the eight essential amino acids.

Modified food starch – usually contains gluten, owing to the manufacturing process; worth checking with the food manufacturer.

Monoglycerides – see **diglycerides**.

Natural flavourings – Check with manufacturers as some natural flavouring contains HVP.

Oats – contain gluten. A few coeliacs are able to tolerate oats; children on the gf/cf diet cannot. Beware the well-meaning health food shop assistant who will assure you that a product is gluten free, even though it contains oats.

Quinoa – (pronounced keen-wa) gf/cf. This is a small, rice-like seed. It contains more protein than any other grain. It is a complete protein with an essential amino acid balance that is close to the ideal. It also provides starch, sugars, oils, fibre, minerals and vitamins. It is easy to digest and makes a good substitute for couscous. Available at health food stores.

Quorn – a meat substitute made from a type of fungi which is bound together with egg. It is gf/cf, as long as it is not part of a ready meal or has been flavoured, both of which may mean it contains gluten and casein. This is not suitable if your child has candida.

Sago – gf/cf. A dry powdered starch from the pith of the sago palm.

Saracen corn – gf/cf. Crushed and hulled buckwheat.

Sesame – gf/cf. This can be in the form of either seeds or flour.

Shoyu – a type of soy sauce. Contains gluten.

Sorghum – gf/cf. Similar to maize.

Soy protein extract – can be gf/cf, but likely to contain MSG. Check with manufacturer.

Spelt – an ancient variety of wheat. Contains gluten.

Starch – can appear on food labels as starch, edible starch, food starch and modified starch. It is used in food processing as a thickener, filler or bulking agent. It can be derived from a number of cereal sources, some of which are gf and some of which contain gluten. The only way to check if it is gluten free is to contact the manufacturer.

Tapioca starch/flour – gf/cf. This is processed cassava root. Also known as cassava, manioc or gari.

Tartaric acid – gf/cf. Another term for cream of tartar.

Texturised protein – usually means texturised soya, which has been used to bulk out the product and cut down on the amount of meat used. Can be gf/cf. It can contain MSG. Worth checking with the manufacturer.

Tofu – soya bean curd, the pressed puree of soya beans. Good protein source. It is gf/cf unless it has been flavoured in any way. You will need to check the ingredients carefully.

Triticale – a variety of wheat. Contains gluten.

TVP/ texturised vegetable protein – developed as a meat substitute for vegetarians. It is soya flour that has been specially processed and dried until it resembles a sponge-like texture. It is gf/cf in its natural state but you will need to check for gluten and casein if it has been flavoured.

Udon – wheat noodles. Contains gluten.

Wheat starch – this has been specially treated to remove gluten from wheat. Commercially produced wheat starch can still have a high residual wheat protein (gluten) content. This should be avoided.

A product that contains wheat starch and also states that it conforms to the **Codex Alimentarius International Gluten-free Standard** is suitable for the gf/cf diet. If your child has a bad reaction to a product that conforms to the above standard, then your child is very sensitive and all such products should be avoided in the future.

Wild rice – gf, unless it is flavoured in any way.

Xanthan gum – gf/cf. Derived from a variety of plant sources. Used widely in gf baking as a 'gluten replacement'. Used throughout the food industry as a stabiliser, thickener and emulsifier.

Yeast, fresh and dried – gf/cf.

Yeast extract – contains naturally occuring MSG.

Further Reading

Medical and scientific studies and research papers

As I have claimed all the way through this book that 'I don't do science', I thought I had better rectify this for those of you who do 'do science' or want to find out more about either the issues that are raised in this book or other related issues. There are a variety of medical and scientific studies and research which deal with the different aspects of the problems that our children can suffer from. The list below is not inclusive, but should provide you with a good basis to progress further, if you should so wish.

Nearly all the papers listed below are available on the Internet; your local library can obtain most, although you may well need to wait for them to order the papers for you. Many of the papers (either in full or in an abridged version) are available from AiA. These I have marked as such. If you have problems obtaining the required paper elsewhere, AiA will be happy to send you a copy. Contact details for AiA are listed in the Directory.

Dr Russell L. Blaylock, 'Food Additive Excitotoxins and Degenerative Brain Disorders.' *The Medical Sentinel*.

Also available from AiA. A very interesting article on the history and effects of excitotoxins. A must-read if you have concerns about monosodium glutamate and aspartame.

J. E. Jan, H. Espezel and R. E. Appleton, 'The Treatment of Sleep Disorders with Melatonin.' *Developmental Medicine and Child Neurology* 36, 1994, 97–100.

Study of the effects of melatonin on the sleep patterns of children with multiple neurological disabilities. Melatonin is naturally produced by the body and may be a better alternative than sedatives for overcoming sleep problems in our children.

Mary N. Megson, MD, FAAP, 'Is Autism a G-Alpha Protein Defect Reversible with Natural Vitamin A?'

Available from AiA. A very readable (i.e. scientific terminology kept to a minimum!) paper, that puts forward the theory that many of the autistic traits are due to certain receptors in the brain being weakened and that natural vitamin A will help to reverse the process. Please note that excessive dosages of vitamin A are acutely toxic. Read the paper before taking any action.

K. L. Reichelt (Institute of Pediatric Research, University of Oslo), A. M. Knisvberg (Centre for Reading Research) and M. Nodland (Madlavoll School, Norway), *The Pathophysiology of Autism Explained?*

Available from AiA. Offers a medical explanation of the many ways that autism can express itself in an individual and how these 'symptoms' are related to the opioid excess theory. Lots of other medical research is used to back up this explanation. These references, if followed up, will keep you reading for days.

Bernard Rimland, PhD, 'Candida Caused Autism.'

The Autism Research Institute, San Diego, USA. Abridged version only available from AiA. Highly recommended and very readable. The title says it all; this paper refers to the effects and occurrence of candida in autistic individuals.

Bernard Rimland PhD, *B6 and Magnesium in the Treatment of Autism.*

The Autism Research Institute, San Diego, USA. An abridged version is available from AiA. The unabridged version is well worth reading. Results of studies carried out since the 1960s, into the use of B6 and magnesium in treating autism.

Bernard Rimland PhD, 'Dimethylglycine (DMG), a Non-toxic Metabolite and Autism.' *Autism Research Review* 4, 2.

Abridged version available from AiA. Relates the study and anecdotal evidence of the use of DMG in the treatment of autism. Very readable.

Paul Shattock, *The Use of Medication for People with Autism.*

Autism Research Unit, Sunderland University, also available from AiA. Discusses the use of drugs in general and focuses upon drugs that are commonly prescribed for autistic people.

Paul Shattock and Dawn Savery, *Urinary Profiles of People with Autism: Possible Implications and Relevance to Other Research.*

Available from the Autism Research Unit, Sunderland University and AiA. Covers the opioid excess theory and the science behind the urinary testing of peptides.

A. J. Wakefield, S. H. Murch, A. Anthony, J. Linnell, D. M. Casson, M. Malik, M. Berelowitz, A. P. Dhillon, M. A. Thomson, P. Harvey, A. Valentine, S. E. Davies, J. A. Walker-Smith, 'Ileal-lymphoid-nodular Hyperplasia, Non-specific Colitis, and Pervasive Developmental Disorder in Children.' *The Lancet* 351, February 28 1998.

Studies at the Royal Free Hospital and the Medical School (London), suggest an inflammatory bowel disease unique to autistic subjects. Links with the MMR vaccination found.

R. H. Waring, *Enzyme and Sulphur Oxidation Deficiencies in Autistic Children with Known Food/Chemical Intolerances.*

Shortened version only available from AiA. Full article appeared in *Journal of Orthomolecular Medicine* 8, 3 December 1993. A very complex study, but well worth reading (the abridged AiA version is easier to digest!). Results of a study to determine whether autistic children who have food and/or chemical intolerances are deficient in phenol-sulphotransferase-P enzyme and/or a low capacity to oxidise sulphur compounds. The study ties in with the opioid excess theory.

Reed P. Warren PhD, Roger A. Burger MS, Dennis Odell MD, Anthony K. Torres MD, Louise Warren RN, 'Decreased Plasma Concentrations of the C4B Complement Protein in Autism.' *Archives of Paediatrics and Adolescent Medicine* 148, February 1994, 180–183.

This study found that autistic subjects have a decreased level of C4B, a component of the immune system. It may well help to explain why so many children's slide into autism occurs after vaccinations or a virus.

Related reading material

Dr Jonathan Brostoff and Linda Gamlin, *Food Allergy and Intolerance.* Bloomsbury Press. ISBN 0 7475 0242 0.

An easy to read book, covering all aspects of food allergies and intolerances.

Maurice Hanssen with Jill Marsden, *E for Additives.* HarperCollins Publishers. ISBN 0 7225 1562 6.

A wonderful book that is straightforward and informative about all E numbers and other food additives. Well researched and readable. Will help you sort out the good additives from the bad and the downright harmful. Comes highly recommended, especially as there are so many lists of 'harmful' additive lists doing the rounds at the moment. If you compare these lists with the information contained in this book you'll realise how wrong most of the lists are.

Lisa Lewis, *Special Diets for Special Kids.* Jessica Kingsley Publishers. ISBN 1 885477 449.

The original book about the gf/cf diet. Invaluable to me and many others when starting the diet. Still constantly referred to in this house. Lisa does 'do science' and she does it very well – even I can understand it! Loads and loads of recipes included too. Although there are areas of overlap with this book, I would still have no hesitation in recommending it, as there are other areas (and recipes) that I do not cover.

Index